Dwelling with Philippians

A Conversation with Scripture through Image and Word

Elizabeth Steele Halstead

Paul Detterman

Joyce Borger

John D. Witvliet

editors

William B. Eerdmans Publishing Company

Grand Rapids, Michigan / Cambridge, U.K.

© 2010 Wm. B. Eerdmans Publishing Co.

All rights reserved

Published 2010 by

Wm. B. Eerdmans Publishing Co.

2140 Oak Industrial Drive N.E., Grand Rapids, Michigan 49505 /

P.O. Box 163, Cambridge CB3 9PU U.K.

www.eerdmans.com

Published in association with the Calvin Institute of Christian Worship, Calvin College

1855 Knollcrest Circle S.E., Grand Rapids, MI 49546-4402

www.calvin.edu/worship

Printed in the United States of America

15 14 13 12 11 10   7 6 5 4 3 2 1

Library of Congress Cataloging-in-Publication Data

Dwelling with Philippians : a conversation with Scripture through image and word /
   Elizabeth Steele Halstead . . . [et al.], editors.
      p.   cm.
   Includes bibliographical references and indexes.
   ISBN 978-0-8028-6618-9 (pbk. : alk. paper)
   1. Bible. N.T. Philippians—Commentaries.   I. Halstead, Elizabeth Steele.
   BS2705.53.D94   2010
   227'.6077—dc22

                        2010031297

Dwelling with Philippians

God of creation,
You make all things,
   and make all things new.
You have put creativity within each of us,
   sometimes dormant,
   often thwarted,
   repeatedly mis-directed.
By your Holy Spirit, fire our imaginations,
   purge them of inhumanity
   and temper them with the compassion of Christ;
that we may fashion instruments of peace,
   tools of conviviality
   and words of beauty;
to the glory of your kingdom.

Donald Elliott, from *The Westminster Collection of Christian Prayer*

Contents

Acknowledgments

We are grateful to many people who made this volume possible:

Betsy Steele Halstead, who sees deeply into the potential of a wide array of artworks, for attention to hundreds of details at every stage of this publication process,

Paul Detterman, whose keen eye for the evangelical witness of Scripture was indispensable for every section of this volume,

Joyce Borger, whose training in both music and theology and experience as editor of Reformed Worship, *helped us bring together the concerns of pastors, musicians, artists, small group leaders, and individual devotional readers through this publication process,*

Scott Hoezee and Randy Beumer, who joined us for textual study and offered provocative insights into the scriptural texts,

Cindy de Jong, Paul Ryan, and Ron Rienstra, for modeling how corporate worship can be strengthened through drawing upon a wide array of artistic gifts,

Anneke Kaai, Steve Prince, Larry Gerbens, Phil Schaafsma, Edgar Boevé, Chris Stoffel Overvoorde, Carl Huisman, Lisa De Boer, Steve Caton, Mark Torgerson, Sandra Bowden, and Jim Fissel, who have helped us learn about the intersection of artwork and Bible interpretation,

Emily Brink, Bert Polman, Roy Hopp, and other veteran members of the Hymn Society, for their dedication to well-crafted congregational song,

Emily Cooper, who worked tirelessly on copyright permissions,

Carrie Steenwyk, who provided editorial support and expert work on the indices,

Nathan Bierma, Emily Brink, Calvin Brondyk, Emily Cooper, Norma de Waal Malefyt, Cindy De Boer, Betty Grit, Betsy Steele Halstead, Bert Polman, Paul Ryan, Greg Scheer, Kathy Smith, Carrie Steenwyk, Howard Vanderwell, Kristen Verhulst, and Anne Zaki, who provided support within the Calvin Institute of Christian Worship,

Aaron Winkle, Mary Hulst, Trygve Johnson, Kate Davelaar, and Todd Cioffi, who prepared the way for this book to be used in campus-wide Bible studies at Calvin College and Hope College,

Tracey Gebbia for her creative and painstaking work in designing this volume,

Jon Pott and Mary Hietbrink for significant assistance in the publication process,

and Lilly Endowment for grant support for several initiatives of the Calvin Institute of Christian Worship.

John D. Witvliet
Calvin Institute of Christian Worship

Dwelling with Scripture

*W*elcome to an unusual commentary and study guide. *Dwelling with Philippians* invites exploration of the remarkable book of Philippians not primarily through historical, theological, or literary analysis, but rather through evocative juxtapositions of texts and images. It is an invitation to offer an unhurried contemplative response to the mystery, beauty, and life-changing power of the text.

The goal of this book is to help us "let the word of Christ dwell in us richly" (cf Col. 3:16) and to allow the text of Philippians to form our imaginations so that we see the world in a deeper, more life-giving way. Dwelling with Scripture trains our capacity for perception, which helps us see more deeply into the truth about God and ourselves. It prompts fresh insight into sin and grace and forms us for a faithful, hospitable, and just way of life. To this end, think of each artwork in this volume as a question ("How does this artwork help us to understanding some aspect of what Paul is communicating?") rather than as a definitive assertion ("This, surely, is what Paul was getting at").

This book is not a substitute for traditional Bible commentaries or study guides. Historical, theological, and literary analyses of the text are each indispensable. But we are convinced that a book like this can be an instructive supplement to these kinds of studies by harnessing the considerable power of artworks to help readers grasp Philippians' gospel message.

Some of the artists represented here did not have any religious intention in the creation of their work. Nevertheless, we sense that their work has great potential to lead us into constructive conversations with the biblical text. These juxtapositions also serve as an invitation to look for other artworks that do the same thing, an invitation that can send each of us out into our daily lives on the lookout for even more striking possibilities.

Other artists represented here produced their work as acts of devotion; some were even created for the purpose of supporting public worship. There is particular emphasis in this book on hymn poems,

---

The entire book of Philippians can be read in about twenty minutes.

And in our workaday world of fast and faster, it may be tempting to approach this letter of Paul in that way. But this little book will help us avoid that temptation. For this small book invites us to sit, to ponder, to look, to listen.

This book is an invitation to rest.

Come apart and rest for a while, Jesus said to his disciples. And he still says that. Come apart—apart from the urgent and the undone, apart from the frantic and the frenzied, apart from all that threatens to pull you apart—Come apart from all those things, and rest.

Hold this book in your hands and read. Read slowly, read out loud, read to someone else. And then gaze upon the images. Look for patterns of light and darkness, look for shifts in color and shade, look for God to teach and to nourish, to encourage and refresh.

Rest. Read. Look. Listen.

God is here. God is here. God is here.

"Let your gentleness be evident to all," says Paul. "The Lord is near."

Enjoy him.

Mary Hulst, Chaplain, Calvin College

Fred Craddock used to say that all preachers need to sit in two chairs each week. The first is the Exegetical Chair. This is a wooden ladder-back chair that requires you to sit up straight. The preacher sits here to do the serious work of digging into a biblical text, unearthing the key points that emerge from a study of the Hebrew, the Greek, the lexicons, the commentaries. There are no shortcuts to doing this kind of hard research. But the second is the Homiletical Chair. This is the La-Z-Boy recliner into which you bring all the fruits of the Exegetical Chair so as to lift those insights up into the light of the imagination. As a preacher, you now know what the text means. Now it's time to do the equally hard work of connecting that text to the lives of the congregation by doing some dreaming, some whimsical free associating, so as to discover just the right image, anecdote, story, or analogy that will bring the text alive for contemporary hearers. If the first chair is where the core message of the text is encountered, the second chair is where that message takes wing into the present moment.

Neither chair exists without the other, and each properly informs the other, too. This book likewise goes both directions. In one sense this book informs the work done in the Homiletical Chair by providing artwork, poetry, hymn selections, and other media that we hope

continued in following box _____

texts written for congregations to sing together. Hymn poetry is a particularly challenging form of poetry to write. Like all poetry, it condenses significant meaning into a relatively small number of words. Unlike some poetry, it is written to be accessible to singers as they sing it the first time. (Hymns that cryptically withhold their message to the last line or which demand careful analysis rarely work for unrehearsed singing in congregations!) Consider using these hymn poems not only for personal reflection but also for corporate worship. A list of suggested tunes can be found at **www.calvin.edu/worship**.

Visual Motifs and Metaphors

As you engage with this book, look for recurring visual motifs and metaphors in both the biblical text and in the artworks. At times, the artworks explore a metaphor in the biblical text; at other times, they explore complementary motifs, commenting on one image by means of another. Here is a sampling of the images you will find:

Tree: From Eden through Calvary to the New Jerusalem, the image of the tree permeates Scripture. Trees can be found throughout this book as well—representing life, fruitfulness, community, protection, and salvation.

Cross: The central symbol of Christians is the symbol of God's promised grace that joins earth to heaven and embraces the world.

Circle: This simple geometric pattern points to assurance and embrace, community and commitment, God's eternity and our security.

Light: Light is a frequent biblical image for revelation, truth, insight, and the banishment of fear. In visual art, both the source and the resting place of light often reveal the artist's message and purpose.

Path: Paul's letter to the Philippians is filled with movement inviting the journey from isolation to community, from self-centeredness to Christ-centeredness, from aimlessness to purposeful mission, from entitlement to joy, from silence to proclamation, from existence in this world to citizenship in God's kingdom.

Dying and Rising: The basic salvation story of Jesus is a story of going down in humiliation and coming up in exaltation. Jesus emptied himself of all glory, came to sinful earth in human form, was killed by human hatred, was raised by divine power, and has now returned to greater glory. Christians experience this same pattern through moment-by-moment dying to sin and rising to life in Christ.

Meal: The Meal, shared among Christians in the pattern Jesus gave, is both a celebration of God's constant proximity and a reminder of God's ultimate promise—that creation, when it is fully and finally restored, will elicit joy and thanksgiving that defy our deepest imagination. Central to biblical Eucharist is like-minded unity—people of one faith gathered around one table for one purpose: to be the good news–proclaiming, miracle-witnessing, disciple-making, community-transforming Body of Christ until he returns.

Vincent van Gogh, *Olive Trees, Pink Sky*, 1889

will set the homiletical imagination on fire. At the same time, however, this set of resources can add to the anticipation with which the preacher approaches also the exegetical task as the research into a text can be seen as existing on a delightful trajectory toward insights and ideas that are fresh and current.

This volume is designed to provide a multiplicity of angles into the text of Philippians that we hope will be both exegetically and homiletically fruitful by providing what preachers so often sorely desire to find: ideas that knock one's thinking sideways. "Tell all the truth," Emily Dickinson famously wrote, "but tell it slant." It's the "slant" part that challenges preachers. Once the preacher knows what the text has to say, the challenge is to help the text speak "slant," to feel fresh in ways that the people in the pews on Sunday morning will understand.

By the grace of the Holy Spirit, the preacher never quite knows what might open up access to that freshness. It may be an image that the preacher had never before associated with a particular passage. It may be re-imagining how the now-famous words spoken by Jesus sounded in the ears of those who heard it all for the very first time. It may be wondering if just possibly the words we always assumed had been originally delivered in a loud, confident voice

continued in following box, next page _____

actually came out in a softer, more tremulous tone.

This is a book to encourage such wonderings. Linger over this volume, sing quietly to yourself the songs that are quoted, recite the psalms and the poems aloud, gaze at the images to wonder if the Spirit will open a whole new set of insights into the text through what is depicted in the painting or the photo. Through this type of engagement with Scripture, that wonderful moment in the sermon-making process may come: the moment when a smile curls up the corners of the preacher's mouth just before he or she says, "Ah-ha . . . I think I now know what I am going to say on Sunday!"

Scott Hoezee, Director,
Center for Excellence in Preaching,
Calvin Theological Seminary

Using this Book

We hope that this will be used in a variety of settings, in both personal and congregational life:

- A small group or Bible study might gather to reflect on how these texts and images engage significant aspects of the biblical text. Questions found at the end of each introduction are designed to stimulate small group discussion.

- Teams that gather to plan worship may use these resources to focus their collective imagination on the nature and beauty of God, the world, and the gospel or, more specifically, to guide their worship planning around a dimension of the biblical text. The volume would especially be useful for planning any service based on a text from Philippians. But given the links between many texts in Philippians and other key biblical themes, the volume can be useful far beyond the services that focus only on Philippians.

- Pastors or teachers may study this commentary on Philippians alongside others while planning a sermon or teaching series on the text of Philippians. Even better, pastors or teachers might challenge members of their congregation or class to use this volume for personal study in conjunction with a sermon or teaching series.

- Teachers or youth leaders could begin a discussion on the text by capturing the creative imagination of children or youth through exploring and wondering about an image with children or young people.

- Groups of artists or aspiring artists might use this volume to discuss which biblical themes need further exploration through artistic expression and how artistic outpourings can best inform, challenge, and deepen reflections on Scripture.

We are particularly interested in asking how the resources gathered here could function to strengthen public worship. Could your congregation sing one of the hymn texts printed here to illuminate a text or theme (with appropriate permissions)? Could your congregation draw upon one of these visual images, printing or projecting it (with appropriate permissions)? The particular possibilities for this will vary widely across the spectrum of congregations.

- Congregations who thrive on artistic creativity, collaborative engagement, and open-ended reflection may eagerly jump into the conversation with personal reflection and suggestions for additional art.
- Congregations who plan worship thematically or center their worship around expository preaching may find resources that stretch and enhance their thematic approach to the letter to the Philippians.
- Congregations whose worship is shaped by the church year and a common lectionary may find fresh life in the interplay of images, texts, and themes with the text of Philippians.
- Congregations with an active or emerging interest in the arts, even where this is largely separate from liturgical applications, will find that the engagement among the arts stimulates meaningful discussions about God, the role of art in the community, and the lived spirituality of the community.
- Congregations who value intergenerational worship may find among the various media tools to nurture conversation among generations or focus divergent interests on the same biblical theme.

Cornelis Monsma, *Where We Meet (Psalm 85:10-11)*, 1999

This book could also find a home in any number of more formal courses, whether in congregations or seminaries. Courses in New Testament, biblical hermeneutics, homiletics, religious art, and worship come to mind as obvious examples.

As you explore these and other uses, may this collection of material help you discover or rediscover the boundless power and intimate beauty of God's Word. In all these potential settings, we hope that the result is not merely renewed appreciation for the arts, or for a particular artwork. We hope that the result is, instead, a more profound experience of God's embrace of us in Jesus Christ. Our prayer, echoing Paul's prayer, is that by engaging this book "your love may overflow more and more with knowledge and full insight to help you to determine what is best, so that in the day of Christ you may be pure and blameless, having produced the harvest of righteousness that comes through Jesus Christ for the glory and praise of God" (Phil. 1:9-11).

The great meaning of the art of painting for human life is finally that artists, each in their own way, not only bring us in contact with relevant realities but also open our eyes to the beauty and characteristic traits of things, and that they teach us to discern structures and to recognize their meaning for human life. We cannot easily overestimate this more implicitly rather than explicitly exercised function of the art of painting.

As art is an expression of the full human being, drawn from the totality of a person's human experience, we will have to include in our judgment of art more than just the consideration of quality . . . and the consideration of clarity . . . so that the meaning, content and function of the artwork has emerged adequately. For an artwork, in its concrete unity of the elements, has to meet first of all the intrinsic artistic norm, and it is impossible to disconnect this . . . from the truth—whether justice is done to the structures and connections in actual reality—and thus from the Truth. The norm for all art may therefore be found formulated in Philippians 4:8.

Hans R. Rookmaaker, *Western Art and the Meanderings of a Culture*, 2002

Timothy R. Botts, *Philippians 4:8*, 2000

Introducing Philippians

*R*epeatedly, throughout the history of the Church, whenever and wherever the Bible is studied and applied to daily life, three important things will happen: people will be converted to saving faith in the Lord Jesus Christ—the Church will grow; individual Christ followers will grow in personal commitment to a life of faith and holiness; and intensified concern for the poor, the outcast, the marginalized, the oppressed, the sick, and the vulnerable will be translated into acts of compassion and of personal sacrifice. The Word of God changes the pattern and the focus of life. Nowhere in Scripture is this more clearly illustrated than in the early days of faith among the residents of Philippi.

Philippi

In the time of the New Testament, Philippi was the leading city in the district called Macedonia. Situated at the eastern end of a fertile valley about ten miles north of the Aegean Sea, Philippi was a major Roman trade link on the Egnatian Way, an east-west thoroughfare that connected ports on the Asiatic and the Aegean Seas with the cities of Asia Minor. The region surrounding Philippi prospered through agriculture, mining, and other forms of industry. Throughout the century before the founding of the Philippian church, significant battles had been fought near Philippi to gain and retain Roman control of the region.

Aware that the Philippians would be deeply disappointed to see Epaphroditus rather than Timothy return, Paul was faced with a serious challenge. How would he cushion this inevitable disappointment? Might Epaphroditus become the object of undeserved criticism? How could he convey his great joy for the church's continual participation in his apostolic ministry while at the same time rebuking them unambiguously for their grave lapse in sanctification? Would he be able to express his heartfelt thanks for their costly offering and yet discourage them from doing it again? And how would he report truthfully his own troubles without intensifying their spirit of discontent? How to help them in this great hour of their need!

The very difficulty of the task that was before the apostle would draw from him, under divine inspiration, a message full of comfort and joy, rebuke and encouragement, doctrine and exhortation.

Moisés Silva, *Philippians*, 2005

View of Philippi's archaeological site from the acropolis. The forum is in the foreground; the market and "Basilica B" are in the background. Photography taken on 12/11/2000 by Marsyas. File licensed under the Creative Commons Attribution ShareAlike 3.0 License, http://creativecommons.org/licenses/by-sa/3.0/

As a Roman citizen, Paul must have strolled in the forum, where statues of Augustus and his family stood, together with monuments to the Julio-Claudian emperors, eminent citizens of the Colonia Augusta Iulia Philippensis, and the local Thracian kings. It was in the forum too that Paul faced the magistrates (*strategoi*), probably in one of the administrative buildings on the west side.

Chaido Koukouli-Chrysantaki, in *Philippi at the Time of Paul and after His Death*, 1998

The location of [a] funerary structure in the center of the city of Philippi indicates the religious character of the heroon; it was probably connected with the cult of the Great Gods on Samothrake and possibly . . . with the Egyptian gods as well. Recent excavations . . . have shown that this heroon (a precinct with a surrounding wall) was still a revered cult center in Roman times and certainly existed when Paul visited Philippi. The site's strong religious character survived when the religion changed; it was here that the first Christian assembly hall, dedicated to Paul, was erected, to be succeeded in the fifth century by the monumental Octagon Church.

Chaido Koukouli-Chrysantaki, in *Philippi at the Time of Paul and after His Death*, 1998

Acts 16:11-15

We set sail from Troas and took a straight course to Samothrace, the following day to Neapolis, and from there to Philippi, which is a leading city of the district of Macedonia and a Roman colony. We remained in this city for some days. On the sabbath day we went outside the gate by the river, where we supposed there was a place of prayer; and we sat down and spoke to the women who had gathered there. A certain woman named Lydia, a worshiper of God, was listening to us; she was from the city of Thyatira and a dealer in purple cloth. The Lord opened her heart to listen eagerly to what was said by Paul. When she and her household were baptized, she urged us, saying, "If you have judged me to be faithful to the Lord, come and stay at my home." And she prevailed upon us.

Acts 20:6

. . . we sailed from Philippi after the days of Unleavened Bread, and in five days we joined them in Troas, where we stayed for seven days.

The city had been founded by Philip, father of Alexander the Great, and it is his name that it bears. It was founded on the site of an ancient city called *Krēnidēs*, a name which means The Wells or Fountains. Philip had founded Philippi in 368 B.C. because there was no more strategic site in all Europe. There is a range of hills which divides Europe from Asia, east from west and just at Philippi that chain of hills dips into a pass so that the city commanded the road from Europe to Asia, since the road must go through the pass. This was the reason that one of the great battles of history was fought at Philippi; for it was here that Antony defeated Brutus and Cassius, and thereby decided the future of the Roman Empire.

William Barclay, *The Letters to the Philippians, Colossians, and Thessalonians*, rev. ed., 1975

2 Corinthians 8:1-4

We want you to know, brothers and sisters, about the grace of God that has been granted to the churches of Macedonia; for during a severe ordeal of affliction, their abundant joy and their extreme poverty have overflowed in a wealth of generosity on their part. For, as I can testify, they voluntarily gave according to their means, and even beyond their means, begging us earnestly for the privilege of sharing in this ministry to the saints . . .

Philippians 1:1

Paul and Timothy, servants of Christ Jesus,
To all the saints in Christ Jesus who are in Philippi, with the bishops and deacons . . .

Philippians 4:15-16

You Philippians indeed know that in the early days of the gospel, when I left Macedonia, no church shared with me in the matter of giving and receiving, except you alone. For even when I was in Thessalonica, you sent me help for my needs more than once.

1 Thessalonians 2:1-2

You yourselves know, brothers and sisters, that our coming to you was not in vain, but though we had already suffered and been shamefully mistreated at Philippi, as you know, we had courage in our God to declare to you the gospel of God in spite of great opposition.

Have you ever longed to receive a letter from someone you love who has traveled far away? When it finally arrived, nothing else mattered until you knew they were all right. Vermeer painted a woman in such a circumstance. The map behind her fills the distance this letter has traveled. Almost praying in her focus, she holds on to the joyful words, "I'm doing fine, I can't wait to see you again, I love you too." Paul gave his brothers and sisters in Philippi the same kind of joyful and pastoral words that say, God will see us through; we share the love of Christ.

Johannes Vermeer, *Woman Reading a Letter*, c.1662-63

Philippian Christ Followers

From its earliest beginnings as a riverbank Bible study, the congregation of Christ followers who gathered in Philippi demonstrated the work of the Holy Spirit. The Apostle Paul's first encounter with the Philippian believers came at a crucial turning point in his ministry. Prevented by the Holy Spirit from preaching in Asia, Paul was redirected once again, this time away from Bithynia. Then God sent him a vision. Paul saw a man from Macedonia calling out to him for help. In obedience to this vision, Paul, Silas, the recent convert Timothy, and Luke followed the Holy Spirit to Macedonia and its leading city.

When they reached Philippi, the apostles found a group of devout women praying on the riverbank. From this humble gathering, a congregation, as diverse as any that could be found in any city church today, was begun. Among these first converts was Lydia, who with her household was praying by the river. A prominent tradeswoman, she immediately opened her home for the gatherings of the new congregation. Another early convert was a slave girl Paul freed from the power of an evil spirit (much to the economic dismay of her owners). Still another was the city jailer who, along with his family and household, was baptized. Together with many others, these believers formed a prayerful, generous, thriving congregation. Although Scripture suggests that Paul returned to Philippi only two more times, his affection for them remained strong.

Paul's Prison Letter

Letters have a life of their own. More than almost any other form of written communication, letters are personalized, written to the eyes of their recipients. Once written, delivered, and read, the mission of most letters is accomplished. Some letters, however, live on. Some from the days of the early Church were incorporated into the fabric of Holy Scripture. Whenever we are invited to open personal letters that have become Scripture, we become part of the community of their intended recipients—a spiritual partnership that transcends time and circumstance. The counsel we find in Scripture's letters is itself

This is the threefold truth
on which our faith depends;
and with this joyful cry
worship begins and ends:
  Christ has died!
  Christ is risen!
  Christ will come again!

Made sacred by long use,
new-minted for our time,
our liturgies sum up
the hope we have in him:
  Christ has died!
  Christ is risen!
  Christ will come again!

On this we fix our minds
as, kneeling side by side,
we take the bread and wine
from him, the Crucified:
  Christ has died!
  Christ is risen!
  Christ will come again!

By this we are upheld
when doubt and grief assails
our Christian fortitude,
and only grace avails:
  Christ has died!
  Christ is risen!
  Christ will come again!

This is the threefold truth
which, if we hold it fast,
changes the world and us
and brings us home at last.
  Christ has died!
  Christ is risen!
  Christ will come again!

Fred Pratt Green, *This Is the Threefold Truth*, 1980

timeless—human condition meeting divine redemption. All have sinned and fallen short of God's glory. All are in need of God's loving grace in Jesus Christ. All can know Christ and the power of his resurrection.

After nearly two thousand years, Paul's words to the Christ followers in Philippi can be understood at face value today. But remembering that Paul was writing these words from the seclusion of house arrest, a result of his refusal to disavow his faith in Jesus Christ, lends significantly more power to each phrase. Post-modern eyes will tend to read Philippians relationally. Paul intended to convey *much* more.

When he wrote, "For to me, living is Christ and dying is gain" (1:21), Paul spoke from his own life experience—from the time he first met the living Christ on the Damascus Road to that moment, when he was facing trial and probable execution. When he wrote, "I want to know Christ and the power of his resurrection and the sharing of his sufferings by becoming like him in his death" (3:10), Paul was not simply recalling the historical Jesus. He was claiming realities of faith, for himself, for those who would receive this letter, and for every Christ follower throughout the centuries. This conviction that he could know Christ and the power of his resurrection formed the foundation of his ability to live in the assurance of God's eternity no matter what the circumstance of his present reality.

When Paul wrote, "I can do all things through [Christ] who strengthens me" (4:13), he was testifying to the absolute Christ-centeredness of his conscious thoughts. And, when in a few more sentences he wrote, "And my God will fully satisfy every need of yours according to his riches in glory in Christ Jesus" (4:19), he was extending the greatest promise of the Christian faith to every believing heart that would ever hear those words, by the power and inspiration of the Holy Spirit.

Life After Death

If there was one central reality for the Apostle Paul, it was his absolute faith in Christ's resurrection, and as a result, his unwavering conviction that the Resurrection changed everything. Sadly, this single-mindedness about the assurance of the central focus of the Good News has been lost in much of the contemporary Church. We are much more eager to identify ourselves as people of justice, or people of compassion, or people of right doctrine than we are as people who can live lives of truth and justice and compassion because Christ's resurrection has given us ultimate life. So focused was Paul's attention that one commentator has written, "All that has been valuable to him, including his own *goodness*, he now considers worthless, something to be left behind in order that he might gain Christ. . . . If we were to be honest, we would have to admit that the Paul of the Epistle to the Philippians is a stranger to us and his Christianity utterly alien to ours."[1]

Paul saw Christ alive in everything. Why is Christ's resurrection so important? Personal investment. Paul was facing trial before an earthly judge, but his heart was fully invested in the trial he (and everyone else) will face before the eternal Judge. In that trial, the verdict has already been delivered, and because of Christ's death and resurrection, all Christ followers have been found innocent. Paul was imprisoned and apart from the congregation he loved, but like his incarceration in Philippi that led to the jailer's conversion, Paul saw his current situation as an opportunity to be a witness to Christ and his gospel. The Philippian Christians had sent a gift of money to help him meet his needs—an immense sacrifice. Even this gift means nothing to Paul except that it represented their growth into maturity of faith and generosity.

Paul was living the joy of the Resurrection. How can this joy be ours? That is the focus of this book—the result of dwelling with Philippians, allowing the worship-related arts that fill the following pages to guide and direct, inform and infuse our individual and

Martin Bulinya, *Untitled*

1 Bruce L. McCormack, introductory essay in Karl Barth, *The Epistle to the Philippians*, 2002

corporate experience of God until, with humility and amazing joy, we begin to understand what it can mean to us to know Christ, yes and the power of his resurrection—dying to this world and rising with our risen Lord.

Audacious Joy

Welcome to a book about joy. Any book conceived around Paul's letter to the Philippian Christ followers cannot help but be joyful. This is not a book about happiness and how to achieve it. It is not about better living through positive thinking, character development, self-actualization, or some other form of emotional *feng shui*. Instead, words of Scripture and the art and artistry they have inspired combine to articulate a deep, abiding, industrial-strength joy so persistent that contemporary eyes may initially find it unusual or even unnerving. This book, like Paul's letter, is about the unique, life-changing joy that can only be ours in Jesus Christ.

In some ways, this is an audacious book. The joy of the Lord, or even the desire for that joy, seems to be a rare commodity in contemporary Western culture, even among devoted Christ followers. How many congregations can you name whose life together exudes effervescent joy? To people who are living without the hunger of hope, this book may appear to be a simple collage of words and images—nothing more. The transformative power of Christian joy—even Resurrection joy—has little impact on a self-contented life. But if you are hungry, if the promised "joy of the Lord" seems frustratingly elusive, if assurance of God's delight in you is sparse and anxiety might as well be your screen name, this book may speak to you.

So make our joy complete by allowing yourself to be drawn into these pages: away from the urgent—into the eternal. Take time to "dwell" with this book. Savor the biblical text. Look deeply into the poetic and the visual images. Allow the Holy Spirit to speak to you of faith, to haunt you with Divine hope, and to convince you of both the possibility and the reality of inestimable joy.

LORD,

Thou hast made Thyself to be ours,

therefore now show Thyself to us in Thy wisdom, goodness and power.

To walk faithfully in our Christian course we need much grace.

Supply us out of Thy rich store.

We need wisdom to go in and out inoffensively before others,

furnish us with Thy Spirit.

We need patience and comfort,

Thou that art the God of consolations bestow it upon us;

for Christ's sake. Amen.

Richard Sibbes (1577-1635), from *A Chain of Prayer Across the Ages*

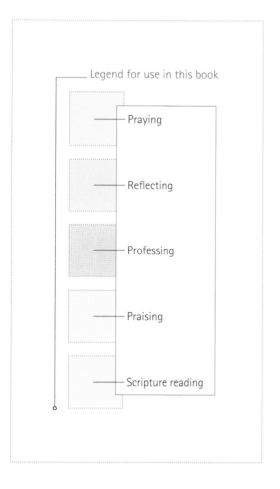

Legend for use in this book

Praying

Reflecting

Professing

Praising

Scripture reading

Don Prys, *Song of the Prairie*, 2004

In addition to these published resources, information and insight for additional reflection and discussion are available at **www.calvin.edu/worship/philippians**. We encourage you to add your insights and comments here as well.

Grace and Peace

Philippians 1:1–2

Philippians 1:1-2

[1]Paul and Timothy, servants of Christ Jesus,

To all the saints in Christ Jesus who are in Philippi, with the bishops and deacons:

[2]Grace to you and peace from God our Father and the Lord Jesus Christ.

I thank my God every time I remember you . . .

In conversation, in correspondence, even in corporate worship, the greeting sets the tone. What is about to happen? What can we expect? What comfort or challenge, good news or bad news are we about to receive?

Paul begins his Philippian letter with a greeting filled with confidence and with the reminder of God's greatest gifts: grace and peace. While this was a common form of greeting in the culture of the New Testament, coming from the Apostle Paul to a community of Christ followers whom he loved, it is no ordinary greeting. In one simple phrase, Paul proclaims the Good News: we are God's people, united and made holy, receiving everything we need from our loving heavenly Father and the One by whom he made himself known to us.

It might seem curious, pious, or simply naive to twenty-first-century people to suggest that God's grace and God's peace are everything we need. If so, this greeting provides our first opportunity to spend some time dwelling in God's presence and in God's Word.

Contemporary people have no difficulty believing we are needy and deserving. We seem hard-wired to believe that no matter how richly we are blessed, we always need more of everything, and we needed it yesterday. Secular people rely on personal drive and ingenuity to provide material possessions, affirmation, gratification, respect, and possibly, if they are lucky, some believable expression of love. Religious people follow the same formula, but instead of relying on personal prowess, they look to their deity of choice to meet these similar expectations. Their god (or gods) reward them for good behavior and punish them when they fail. No matter the source of our fulfillment, each one of us keeps a mental inventory of the proof of our success in relation to the people around us. We feel superior to some and envious of others.

A cursory reading of Paul's greeting, apart from its context in Scripture, might inspire us to think, "Grace; peace; whatever." But when we remember that this letter is part of the epic biblical story, these words become hyperlinks to the Good News! What makes this simple greeting so profound? The realization that good intentions, personal ingenuity, occasional good behavior, even sporadic flirting with prayer and pious living mean nothing to God and have earned us nothing from God.

Long ago, we were created in God's own image, to live in an intimate relationship with God. But we turned away from God, and like a stubborn child who insists on breaking a toy rather than letting you help her put it together, we have never turned back. Grace is God's unconditional invitation to return to the embrace of the Father who patiently waits for obstinate children to want to come home. The more we realize how stubborn and self-made we are, how much we aren't who God created us to be, the greater, the costlier, and the more amazing God's gift of grace becomes. We deserve nothing except God's contempt and condemnation—to be written off by God as a good argument against free will. That fact that we are not dismissed by God, but instead are wooed with endless patience, unconditionally loved, and received with unabashed joy, even while we are still hopelessly less than God created us to be: that is Grace.

When Paul greets Christ followers of any culture with God's grace and in God's peace, it is a reminder that while we were still rebelling—running away—God became one of us, broke our stubborn disobedience, healed the relationship we had destroyed, and now continues to assure us that this restoration is an eternal reality.

It was only because of God's grace that Saul of Tarsus could now write in love to Christ followers whom he used to persecute. And it is only because of God's peace that we can overcome our pride and our envy, be welcomed back into the family of God, and realize the blessing of eternal love, even as we meditate on these simple words.

These gifts from God will always come in this order: grace, then peace. Only when we begin to receive God's grace can we begin to experience the second amazing gift—peace that comes from living as forgiven people—imitating God's grace more and more in our human relationships because we have first received God's grace as a personal blessing. This was Paul's greeting to those he loved—Good News.

Every Christ follower's commission is to emulate Paul and Timothy as they imitate Jesus Christ, remembering that even the most dissonant of God's people can leave the stubborn pursuit of a self-made life, be freed from feeling superior to some and envious of others. God greets us each day, welcoming us into a daily experience of Grace and Peace, of Love and Joy.

1. *How would you have defined "grace" and "peace" before beginning this book?*

2. *Where do you hear the words "grace" and "peace" in contemporary usage? What attributes does our culture honor as "gracious" or "peaceful"?*

3. *Have you experienced God's grace in your life? How?*

4. *In what ways might your understanding and personal experience of God's grace impact your relationship with other people in the Church or in the world?*

5. *Explore the definition of* shalom *(peace) in Scripture. What does God's shalom include?*

6. *What would a group of people who understand and seek God's shalom expect from one another? What would such a unique group of people offer to the world?*

Paul does lay claim to one title. He claims to be the servant (*doulos*) of Christ . . . but *doulos* means more than *servant*, it is *slave*. A servant is free to come and go; but a slave is the possession of his master for ever.

William Barclay, *The Letters to the Philippians, Colossians, and Thessalonians,* 1957, rev. 1975

You can tell a lot about a letter by the way a person signs it. Paul signs Philippians, "Paul and Timothy, slaves of Jesus Christ." Already you know: this is a letter about humility.

Thomas G. Long, "Saints," 1996

Preachers of the God of grace,
heralds of the dawning day—
fit them, Lord, for all they face,
prove their calling, guide their way.
Meeting failure or success,
keep their faith and vision sure,
agents of your righteousness,
trained for unremitting war.

Undeterred by praise or blame,
dear to God, on earth unknown,
zealous for your holy name,
making known what you have done:
constant testing they endure,
persecution, pain and blood;
by your Spirit keep them pure,
fill them with the love of God.

In their weakness, Lord, be strong,
Satan's claims let them destroy;
in their sorrows let their song
be of Christ, their hope and joy.
Fools for you—yet make them wise,
though on them all spite is poured
by a world that crucifies
faithful prophets of the Lord.

Dying daily, let them live;
fainting, make their spirits bold;
empty, teach them still to give;
poor, they shall enrich the world.
Triumph, Lord, when we despair,
honor those whom kings despise:
make their work your church's prayer,
grant your glory as their prize.

Christopher M. Idle, *Preachers of the God of Grace,* 1976

Randy Beumer, *Written in Shackles,* 2006

6

I speak to you who have just been reborn in baptism, my little children in Christ, you who are the new off-spring of the church, gift of the Father, proof of Mother Church's fruitfulness. All of you who stand fast in the Lord are a holy seed, a new colony of bees, the very flower of our ministry and fruit of our toil, my joy and my crown.

Augustine (354–430)

Communion of Saints, Cathedral of Our Lady of the Angels, Los Angeles, California, 2001-02

For all the saints who showed your love
in how they lived and where they moved,
for mindful women, caring men,
accept our gratitude again.

For all the saints who loved your name,
whose faith increased the Savior's fame,
who sang your songs and shared your word,
accept our gratitude, good Lord.

For all the saints who named your will,
and saw your kingdom coming still
through selfless protest, prayer and praise,
accept the gratitude we raise.

Bless all whose will or name or love
reflects the grace of heaven above.
Though unacclaimed by earthly powers,
your life through theirs has hallowed ours.

John L. Bell, *For All the Saints Who Showed Your Love*, 1989

The people at Corinth assumed that sainthood was a position of moral status. It was a destination to which a person of moral perfection arrived. That's what it meant to be a saint. To which Paul says, "No. Sainthood is not a destination. It's a journey. You were called to be saints." . . . [A saint is] a baptized person with a vocation.

Thomas G. Long, "Saints," 1996

The designation of the Philippians as the holy [ones] in Christ Jesus describes the condition in which they find themselves on the ground of a specific mind and attitude towards them on God's part (not vice versa!) . . . 'Holy' people are unholy people, who nevertheless as such have been singled out, claimed, and requisitioned by God for his control, for his use, for himself who is holy. Their holiness is and remains in Christ Jesus.

Karl Barth, *The Epistle to the Philippians*, 1947

Isaiah 62:12
They shall be called, "The Holy People, The Redeemed
   of the LORD";
and you shall be called, "Sought Out, A City Not
   Forsaken."

. . . Our task as the covenant community, the church,
is to be God's temple, so filled with his glorious
presence that we expand and fill the earth with that
presence until God finally accomplishes the goal
completely at the end of time!

G. K. Beale, *The Temple and the Church's Mission*, 2004

When I use the word "saint" I'm using it not in the
cultural sense of someone who is holier than other
people; I'm using it in the theological sense of a
baptized member of the Christian community. As a
matter of fact, that understanding of a person as a
saint works against the cultural notion of a person as
a saint: Because I am a baptized saint, I can stand up
on Sunday morning and tell the truth about myself
in the prayer of confession . . . without fear that it
will undermine my sacred identity, because it is not
an identity that is earned by being better than other
people, it's one that is given to me by participating in
the reality of Jesus Christ.

Thomas G. Long, "Accompany Them with Singing," 2007

Into the alleys
Into the byways
Into the streets
And the roads
And the highways
Past rumor mongers
And midnight ramblers
Past the liars and the cheaters
   and the gamblers
On Your word
On Your word.
On the wonderful word of the
   Son of God.
I'm stepping out on Your word.

Maya Angelou, excerpt, "Just Like Job," from *The
Complete Collected Poems of Maya Angelou*, 1994

In this image, the shadows falling down from the pews during an April–May sun onto the aisle/street . . . reinforce the phenomenon of the interchangeability of the design from microcosm to macrocosm, with the geometrics of both systems fitting together, in fact echoing each other.

Scott Mutter, *Surrational Images*, 1992

Scott Mutter, *Untitled (Church Aisle)*, 1986

Grace to you and peace *from God our Father and the Lord Jesus Christ.*

Deep peace of the
running wave to you
Deep peace of the
flowing air to you
Deep peace of the quiet
earth to you
Deep peace of the
shining stars to you
Deep peace of the Son
of peace to you

Iona Community, from *The Edge of Glory*, 1985

Makoto Fujimura, *Grace Foretold*, 1998

Jeremiah 29:7
Also, seek the peace and prosperity
of the city to which I have carried
you into exile. Pray to the LORD for
it, because if it prospers, you too will
prosper. *NIV*

Psalm 85:10-14
Salvation is coming near,
glory is filling our land.

Love and fidelity embrace,
peace and justice kiss.
Fidelity sprouts from the earth,
justice leans down from heaven.

The Lord pours out riches,
our land springs to life.
Justice clears God's path,
justice points the way.

The Psalter

Paul translated "grace" into something that evokes the deepest joy
and the greatest thanksgiving because of the wondrous fact that it is
a gift. Not only do we not deserve it, but we could never deserve it—
it cannot be earned but only received. Gracious people, in Paul's view,
are not those who are naturally charming or who have racked up
sufficient merits so as to warrant a god's favor. No, gracious people
are first of all "graced people," that is, people who are gracious in
imitation of God only because they had first been given God's grace
as a sheer, undeserved, surprise gift!

That grace is a gift must be our starting point in trying to understand
"grace" as Paul understood and developed it.

Scott Hoezee, *The Riddle of Grace*, 1996

Thou hidden source of calm repose,
thou all-sufficient love divine,
my help and refuge from my foes,
secure I am, if thou art mine:
and lo! From sin and grief and shame
I hide me, Jesus, in thy name.

Thy mighty name salvation is,
and keeps my happy soul above;
comfort it brings, and pow'r and peace
and joy and everlasting love;
to me, with thy dear name, are giv'n
pardon and holiness and heav'n.

Jesus, my all in all thou art;
my rest in toil, my ease in pain,
the medicine of my broken heart,
in war my peace, in loss my gain,
my smile beneath the tyrant's frown,
in shame my glory and my crown:

In want my plentiful supply,
in weakness my almighty pow'r,
in bonds my perfect liberty,
my light in Satan's darkest hour,
my help and stay whene'er I call,
my life in death, my heav'n, my all.

Charles Wesley, *Thou Hidden Source of Calm Repose*, 1749

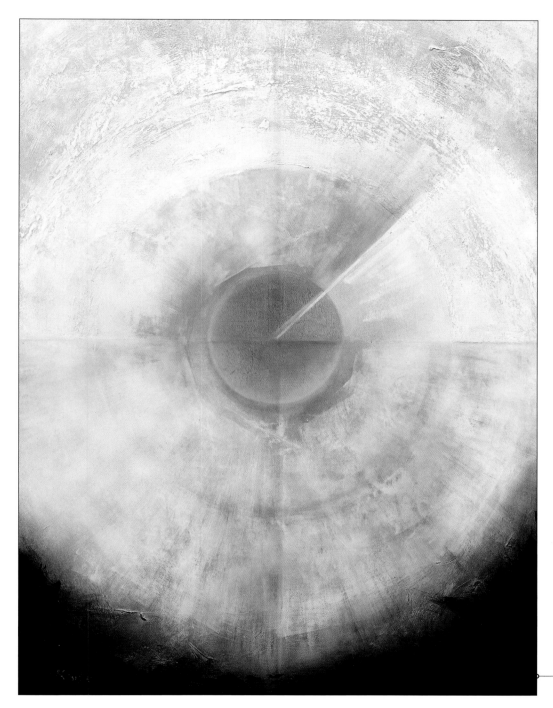

There can be no true peace, where there is not true grace; and where grace goeth before, peace will follow.

Matthew Henry (1662-1714), *Matthew Henry's Concise Commentary on the Bible*

The heart of the light, round shape here symbolizes the inner person, the white band above pictures God, and the shape below refers to the surrounding world. This simple composition expresses a peaceful, orderly rest (*eirene* in Greek). Through Christ, peace with God and the environment is possible, which is why the cross dominates the composition. The inner peace that results is pictured as a rising sun (the moment of peace in nature). Its gentle light softens the harsh contradictions in our world.

Anneke Kaai and Eugene H. Peterson, *In a Word*, 2003

Anneke Kaai, *Peace*, 2003

Confident Prayer

Philippians 1:3-11

Philippians 1:3-11

[3]I thank my God every time I remember you, [4]constantly praying with joy in every one of my prayers for all of you, [5]because of your sharing in the gospel from the first day until now. [6]I am confident of this, that the one who began a good work among you will bring it to completion by the day of Jesus Christ. [7]It is right for me to think this way about all of you, because you hold me in your heart, for all of you share in God's grace with me, both in my imprisonment and in the defense and confirmation of the gospel. [8]For God is my witness, how I long for all of you with the compassion of Christ Jesus. [9]And this is my prayer, that your love may overflow more and more with knowledge and full insight [10]to help you to determine what is best, so that in the day of Christ you may be pure and blameless, [11]having produced the harvest of righteousness that comes through Jesus Christ for the glory and praise of God.

There are different kinds of prayer: adoration, confession, thanksgiving and celebration, heartache and lament—all with biblical roots, and all acceptable conversation, part of an honest relationship among God and his people. There are also many attitudes of prayer. Sometimes God's people pray with hope, sometimes in despair, sometimes with passion, sometimes out of fear. Sometimes we simply pray, "God, please just *do something*."

Paul prayed with confidence for the Christ followers in Philippi who had experienced God's grace and were attempting to live in Christ's peace. They were partners with Paul in ministry. Their friendship, camaraderie, and support contributed to his joy. More importantly, Paul knew that what God had begun in Philippi would not be abandoned or neglected until that good work was brought to full completion for God's purpose.

So, Paul prayed with confident love—love for God and love for God's people. He prayed that the Philippian Christ followers would continue growing in their understanding of their special relationship they enjoyed with God. God loved these people and they knew it. But *knowledge* of God's love was just the beginning. Awareness needed to deepen into discernment of God's purpose and commitment to God's commission.

The important progression from awareness to commitment must not be too quickly overlooked by God's people in any time or place. This is basic discipleship: living as Christ followers in response to the reality of God's presence and awareness of God's purpose within whatever context we find ourselves—because of what God has begun in us before we even knew God was at work.

In one of the *Chronicles of Narnia*, C. S. Lewis tells the story of Shasta, a boy from an isolated fishing village who set out on a great adventure. As with all truly great adventures, Shasta's journey was both thrilling and terrifying. It was during one of the most terrifying times that we join the story. Shasta has discovered he is not alone as he rides along a frightening path. Lewis writes:

> It was pitch dark and [Shasta] could see nothing. And the Thing (or Person) was going so quietly that he could hardly hear any footfalls. What he could hear was breathing. His invisible companion seemed to breathe on a very large scale, and Shasta got the impression that it was a very large creature. And he had come to notice this breathing so gradually that he really had no idea how long it had been there. . . . The Thing (unless it was a Person) went on beside him so very quietly that Shasta began to hope he had only imagined it. But just as he was becoming quite sure of it, there suddenly came a deep, rich sigh out of the darkness beside him. . . . "Who are you?" he said, scarcely above a whisper. "One who has waited long for you to speak," said the Thing. . . .[1]

The companion was Aslan, the great Lion who is the embodiment of Christ. Aslan recounts for Shasta all the times and scenes when, though Shasta had no clue, Aslan was looking out for him; moving undiscerned through Shasta's adventure: a good work faithfully being completed.

Centuries after Paul and before C. S. Lewis, Ignatius Loyola, the founder of the Society of Jesus, wrote of "finding God in all things in order that we might love and serve God in all things." Confident discipleship requires discernment, practiced identification of the trajectory of God's plan and purpose. This too is part of Paul's prayer—that those who know God's presence and are assured of God's love are also confidently expectant that they are part of something far larger than their own life or experience.

Ruth Haley Barton has recently identified three beliefs necessary for the proper discerning of God's work and God's purpose in our lives. First is the *"belief in the goodness of God . . . , that God's will [for us] is the best thing that could happen . . . under any circumstance."* This belief will be the key to considering our next chapter. The second belief Barton identifies in the process of Christian discernment is "that *love is our primary calling."* This is *agape* love; not the emotion of romance, or of friendship, or even of parental affection, but commitment to actively seek the best interest of other people over our own. Scripture is overflowing with the call to *agape*. Finally, if we are to discern what God has begun in our lives, we must believe Jesus' promise of the Spirit as the Interpreter of the demands of *agape* love in any situation.[2]

Paul's goal is a "harvest of righteousness that comes through Jesus Christ for the glory and praise of God" (1:11), strong evidence of the truth of the Good News to a broken and cynical world. In the words of Jesus:

> I'm praying not only for them
> but also for those who will believe in me
> because of them and their witness about me.
> The goal is for all of them to become one heart
>   and mind—
> just as you, Father, are in me and I in you,
> so they might be one heart and mind with us.
> Then the world might believe that you, in fact, sent me.
> The same glory you gave me, I gave them,
> so they'll be as unified and together as we are—
> I in them and you in me.
> Then they'll be mature in this oneness,
> and give the godless world evidence
> that you've sent me and loved them
> in the same way you've loved me.[3]

1 C. S. Lewis, *The Horse and His Boy*, 1954

2 Ruth Haley Barton, *Sacred Rhythms*, 2006

3 John 17:20-23 (Eugene H. Peterson, *The Message*, 2002)

1. *Have you ever had the experience of someone praying specifically for you? How did that make you feel?*

2. *Read Romans 8:34. Notice that Christ's prayer for his people is ongoing. Is the reality of Christ continuously praying for you part of your conscious experience of life?*

3. *When you pray, what percentage of your prayer is focused on talking to God, and what percentage is focused on listening for God and discerning God's will?*

4. *Can you think of a specific example in your life when God's will proved to be best for you despite the circumstances of the moment?*

5. *Agape is at the heart of the Christian faith. Agape is love for others not based on relationship, physical or emotional desire, or attraction, but simply caring about others more than self and wanting the best for them. Have you experienced this kind of love?*

6. *Would it surprise you to know that God's will for you is to experience and express God's agape? How, specifically, would your life be different if each day was shaped by this understanding of God's will?*

I thank my God *every time I remember you,* constantly **praying with joy** . . .

What do you understand by "the communion of saints"?

First, that all and every one, who believes, being members of Christ, are in common, partakers of him, and of all his riches and gifts; secondly, that every one must know it to be his/her duty, readily and cheerfully to employ his/her gifts, for the advantage and salvation of other members.

The Heidelberg Catechism, 1563

And I also rejoice because the firm root of your faith, famous from the earliest times, still abides and bears fruit for our Lord Jesus Christ, who endured for our sins even to face death.

Polycarp, *The Letter of Saint Polycarp, Bishop of Smyrna, to the Philippians*, early second century

Bernadette Lopez, *Je crois à la communion des saints*, 2003

Don Prys, *Song of the Prairie*, 2004

Paul pleaded and prayed to God in the joyful remembrance of his friends. These prayers are like a tune that spans the horizon of creation. In Don Prys's piece, joyful notes dance across a map. They sing the tune above the prairie to suggest a reason for rejoicing in creation and relationships. Wherever we are we can listen to and play, as Paul did, the joyful music of good memories.

Let songs of thanksgiving and glad psalms of praise
    resound through the heavens extolling God's ways,
for since our faith journey began long ago,
    our God has been with us and helped us to grow.

Give thanks for the people who, led by God's grace,
    had vision to gather a church in this place.
Sing praise for their mission, and all they endured
    to be Christ's disciples and God's living Word.

Give thanks for the faithful who walk in their way,
    still led by a vision of mission today
to care for the homeless, the hungry and ill,
    the prisoner and stranger, with love and good will.

Give thanks for our children and gifts that they bring,
    their joy in God's presence, the songs that they sing.
As they learn to worship, and study, and pray,
    the church of tomorrow is born here today.

Sing praise for the journey of faith that we share.
    Sing praise, and be thankful for God's love and care.
Rejoice in Christ Jesus, who walks at our side,
    and hope in the Spirit, our Light and our Guide.

Mary Nelson Keithahn, *Sing Praise for the Journey*, 2000

O Lord our God, we thank you
for the many people throughout the ages
who have followed your way of life joyfully:
for the many saints and martyrs, men and women,
who have offered up their very lives
so that your life abundant may become manifest
and your kingdom may advance.

**For your love and faithfulness
we will at all times praise your name.**

O Lord, we thank you for those
who chose the way of your Son, our brother Jesus
    Christ.
In the midst of trial, they held out hope;
in the midst of hatred, they kindled love;
in the midst of persecutions, they witnessed to your
    power;
in the midst of despair, they clung to your promise.

**For your love and faithfulness
we will at all times praise your name.**

O Lord, we thank you for the truth they learned
and passed on to us:
that it is by giving that we shall receive;
it is by becoming weak that we shall be strong;
it is by loving others that we shall be loved;
it is by offering ourselves that the kingdom will
    unfold;
it is by dying that we shall inherit life everlasting.
Lord, give us courage to follow your way of life.

**For your love and faithfulness
we will at all times praise your name. Amen.**

World Council of Churches, *Jesus Christ the Life of the World*, 1983

I am confident of this, that the one who began a good work among you will **bring it to completion** . . .

1:6

Timothy R. Botts, *Philippians 1:6*, 2000

A debtor to mercy alone,
of covenant mercy I sing;
nor fear, with your righteousness on,
my person and off'ring to bring.
The terrors of law and of God
with me can have nothing to do;
my Savior's obedience and blood
hide all my transgressions from view.

The work which his goodness began,
the arm of his strength will complete;
his promise is yea and amen,
and never was forfeited yet.
Things future, nor things that are now,
nor all things below or above,
can make him his purpose forgo,
or sever my soul from his love.

My name from the palms of his hands
eternity will not erase;
impressed on his heart it remains,
in marks of indelible grace.
Yes, I to the end shall endure,
as sure as the earnest is giv'n;
more happy, but not more secure,
the glorified spirits in heav'n.

Augustus M. Toplady, *A Debtor to Mercy Alone*, 1771

There are many times we think we love you well, O God.
But upon hearing your call to love you with all our heart,
and all our mind, and all our strength,
we confess that our love for you is a diluted love,
made insipid and flat by lesser loyalties and a divided
   heart.
Our love seems pure only for brief moments;
soon our affections are drawn away.
How easily our devotion dies.
Forgive us;
in deep mercy spare us, despite our lost first love for you;
in grace rekindle our love for you
in seeing anew Jesus' love for us. Amen.

Kenneth Koeman, from *Reformed Worship*, 1993

*. . . all of you **share in God's grace** with me, both in **my imprisonment** and in the defense and confirmation of the gospel. . . .*

. . . A painting . . . that may present the most human St. Paul in art. . . . Here, then, is an old Paul: no halos, no angels, no piercing holy genius glare, just an old man surrounded by his books, one shoe kicked off to relieve what looks like a bunioned foot and toes with corns, paper at the ready, pen in hand, and that thinking look beyond where he is into the nearness of how to write down what he feels. It is not the look of writer's block, but the struggle to express a reality too large for mere words.

John I. Durham, *The Biblical Rembrandt*, 2004

Rembrandt Harmensz. van Rijn, *Saint Paul in Prison*, 1627

O Lord:

In a world where many are lonely,
we thank you for our friendships.

In a world where many are captive,
we thank you for our freedom.

In a world where many are hungry,
we thank you for your provision.

We pray that you will:
enlarge our sympathy,
deepen our compassion,
and give us grateful hearts.

In Christ's name.

Terry Waite, from *Prayers Encircling the World*, 1998

His chains are without doubt a *confirmation of the gospel*. How? Because if he had refused the bonds, he would have been seen as a deceiver. But the one who endures everything, including persecution and imprisonment, shows that he does not suffer them for any human reason but on account of God, who rights the balance. . . . See how absolutely he turns everything on its head. For what others might view as a weakness or reproach, this he calls *confirmation*.

St. John Chrysostom (c. 347–407), *Homily on Philippians ii.1.7*

From your hand, O Lord, we receive
everything.
You stretch your powerful hand, and
turn worldly wisdom into holy
folly.
You open your gentle hand, and offer
the gift of inward peace.
If sometimes it seems that your arm is
shortened,
then you increase our faith and trust,
so that we may reach out to you.
And if sometimes it seems that you
withdraw your hand from us,
then we know that it is only to
conceal the eternal blessing which
you have promised—
that we may yearn even more
fervently for that blessing.

Søren Kierkegaard (1813-1855), *Selected Readings*

We are the singers who celebrate Jesus,
we are the cast of a play to unfold,
we have a part at the heart of the Gospel,
action that speaks as the Story is told,

we are God's people, hopeful and joyful,
one open circle round Jesus Christ!

This is the wonder, that we should be chosen!
We, like the earthenware vessels we are,
clay in a mold to enfold the great treasure:
light of more power than sunburst or star, *refrain*

We are the travellers set on a voyage,
ship that will sail with whoever will board,
we who can dream a regime of acceptance,
seeking a country of loving accord, *refrain*

We have a life that is greening and growing,
centered on Jesus, the root and the vine,
we are a place for each race and each rainbow,
household of faith with a pledge of new wine, *refrain*

Shirley Erena Murray, *We Are the Singers*

Lisa Ellis, *Miriam's Dance*, 2006

*And this is my prayer, that your love may overflow more and more with knowledge and full insight to help you to **determine what is best** . . .*

Discernment and choices are interconnected themes
   within this piece . . .
— Holding hands, cut from a printed map, to the
   heart
— The sky unfolding a new vision
— Below, winding paths of unique choices . . .

Merciful God,
you made us in your image,
with a mind to know you,
a heart to love you,
and a will to serve you.
But our knowledge is imperfect,
our love inconstant,
our obedience incomplete.
Day by day we fail to grow into your
   likeness;
yet you are slow to be angry with
   your children.
For the sake of Jesus Christ,
your Son, our Savior,
do not hold our sins against us,
but in your tender love, forgive.

Lord have mercy.
Christ have mercy.
Lord have mercy.

Book of Common Order of the Church of Scotland, 1994

Jan L. Richardson, *Wisdom's Path*, 1998

28

Discernment or prudence, says Augustine, "is love distinguishing with sagacity [wisdom] between what hinders it and what helps it. . . . Prudence is love making a right distinction between what helps it towards God and what might hinder it."

Augustine (354-430), *The Writings against the Manicheans, and against the Donatists*

1 Kings 3:9
Give your servant therefore an understanding mind to govern your people, able to discern between good and evil; for who can govern this your great people?

Romans 12:2
Do not be conformed to this world, but be transformed by the renewing of your minds, so that you may discern what is the will of God—what is good and acceptable and perfect.

Merciful God,
in your tender love, forgive us
and cause our love for you to abound
more and more in knowledge and depth of insight,
so that we may be able to discern what is best
and may be pure and blameless until the day of
   Christ, filled with the fruit of righteousness
that comes through Jesus Christ,
to your glory and praise. Amen.

Paul Detterman, 2005; Phil. 1:9-11, NIV

At the heart of this prayer is Paul's desire that his readers exercise the classical virtue of discernment. He wants them to be able to make good choices, to "determine what is best." In his prayer, Paul gives us the anatomy of this virtue. He points to three necessary building blocks for discernment: love, knowledge, and insight. He also describes the desired result of exercising this virtue: holiness and righteousness that will contribute to the glory and praise of God. In this way, the virtue of discernment energizes and empowers the thoughtful, mature Christian life.

John D. Witvliet, *Worship Seeking Understanding*, 2003

. . . so that . . . you may be pure and blameless, having produced the **harvest of righteousness** *. . .*

Gustav Klimt, *Pear Tree,* 1903

Klimt, Gustav (1862-1918). Pear Tree. 1903 (later reworked). Oil on canvas, 101 x 101 cm (39 3/4 x 39 3/4 in.). Gift of Otto Kallir, BR66.4. Photo: Katya Kallsen. Busch-Reisinger Museum, Harvard Art Museum, Cambridge, Massachusetts, U.S.A. © Harvard Art Museum / Art Resource, NY.

Philippians 1:11
. . . having produced the harvest of righteousness that comes through Jesus Christ for the glory and praise of God.

Philippians 4:18
I have been paid in full and have more than enough; I am fully satisfied, now that I have received from Epaphroditus the gifts you sent, a fragrant offering, a sacrifice acceptable and pleasing to God.

Paul's desire that the people be ever more fruitful is a theme running through the Old and New Testaments:

Psalm 1:3
They are like trees planted by streams of water,
which yield their fruit in its season, and their leaves do not wither.
In all that they do, they prosper.

Isaiah 32:15-20
When the Spirit is given to us from heaven, deserts will become orchards thick as fertile forests. Honesty and justice will prosper there, and justice will produce lasting peace and security. You, the LORD's people, will live in peace, calm and secure, even if hail-stones flatten forests and cities. You will have God's blessing, as you plant your crops beside streams, while your donkeys and cattle roam freely about. *CEV*

Colossians 1:6, 10
. . . Just as [hope] is bearing fruit and growing in the whole world, so it has been bearing fruit among yourselves from the day you heard it and truly comprehended the grace of God. . . . so that you may lead lives worthy of the Lord, fully pleasing to him, as you bear fruit in every good work and as you grow in the knowledge of God.

Hebrews 12:11
Now, discipline always seems painful rather than pleasant at the time, but later it yields the peaceful fruit of righteousness to those who have been trained by it.

Revelation 22:1-2
Then the angel showed me the river of the water of life, bright as crystal, flowing from the throne of God and of the Lamb through the middle of the street of the city. On either side of the river is the tree of life with its twelve kinds of fruit, producing its fruit each month; and the leaves of the tree are for the healing of the nations.

Philippians 2:12b-13a

. . . work out your own salvation with fear and trembling; for it is
God who is at work in you . . .

All farmers know that there is always more work to be done than there is time to do
it; nevertheless, these same farmers also understand that much of what happens to
the crops is beyond their control. There is much for the farmer to do, but the farmer
cannot make the seed sprout, the sun shine or the rain fall. In fact, it is only because
the farmer trusts that these good gifts will *continue* to be given that the challenging
and risk-filled enterprise of farming is undertaken at all. Grace and effort, gift and
work: these must be held together. Unfortunately, Christians often either pit these
against each other or emphasize one to the exclusion of the other. The wisdom of the
farmer reminds us that both are required, in full measure, in order to grow anything
worth harvesting. The same holds for the life of the Spirit.

Philip D. Kenneson, *Life on the Vine*, 1999

Speak, O Lord, as we come to you, to receive the food of your holy Word.
Take your truth, plant it deep in us; shape and fashion us in your likeness,
that the light of Christ might be seen today in our acts of love and our deeds of faith.
Speak, O Lord, and fulfill in us all your purposes for your glory.

Teach us, Lord, full obedience, holy reverence, true humility.
Test our thoughts and our attitudes in the radiance of your purity.
Cause our faith to rise, cause our eyes to see your majestic love and authority.
Words of power that can never fail—let their truth prevail over unbelief.

Speak, O Lord, and renew our minds; help us grasp the heights of your plans for us—
truths unchanged from the dawn of time, that will echo down through eternity.
And by grace we'll stand on your promises; and by faith we'll walk as you walk with us.
Speak, O Lord, 'til your church is built, and the earth is filled with your glory.

Keith Getty and Stuart Townend, *Speak, O Lord*

© See Text Sources

*Being filled with the
fruits of righteousness,
which are through Jesus
Christ, to the glory and
praise of God*—Here
are three properties of
that sincerity which is
acceptable to God: It
must bear fruits, the
fruits of righteousness,
all inward and
outward holiness, all
good tempers, words,
and works; and that
so abundantly, that
we may be filled with
them. The branch and
the fruits must derive
both their virtue and
their very being from
the all-supporting, all-
supplying root, Jesus
Christ. As all these
flow from the grace of
Christ, so they must
issue in the glory and
praise of God.

John Wesley, *Explanatory Notes
Upon the New Testament*, 1755

Eric Nykamp, *Grow Where You Are Planted*, 2002

*. . . the harvest of righteousness that comes through Jesus Christ for the **glory** and **praise** of God.*

John August Swanson, *Psalm 85*, 2003

"THERE is no 'afterward' on earth for me!"
  Beloved, 'tis not so!
That God's own "afterwards" are pledged to thee,
  Thy life shall show.

No "afterward" indeed of great things wrought,
  By willing hands and feet;
No sheaf is thine, from wider harvests brought,
  With singing sweet.

Fair flowing years of ease and laughing strength,
  With cloudless morning skies,
Sweet life renewed, and active work at length,
  His love denies.

But living fruit of righteousness to Him
  His chastening shall yield,
And constant "afterwards," no longer dim,
  Shall be revealed.

Is it no "afterward" that in thy heart
  His *love* is shed abroad?
And that His Spirit breathes, while called apart,
  The *peace* of God?

That *joy* in tribulation shall spring forth
  To greet His visits blessed,
Whose wisdom wakes the south wind or the north,
  As He sees best!

Shall not *longsuffering* in Thee be wrought,
  To mirror back His own!
His *gentleness* shall mellow every thought,
  And look, and tone.

And *goodness*! In thyself dwells no good thing,
  Yet from thy glorious Root
An "afterward" of holiness shall spring—
  Most precious fruit!

The trial of thy *faith* from hour to hour
  Shall yield a grand increase;
He shall fulfil the work of faith with power
  That cannot cease.

And all around shall praise Him as they see
  The *meekness* of thy Lord.
Thus, even here and now, how blest shall be
  Thy sure reward!

This pleasant fruit it shall be thine to lay
  At thy Belovèd's feet,
The ripening clusters growing day by day
  More full and sweet.

If at His gate He keeps thee waiting now
  Through many a suffering year,
Watch for His daily "afterwards," and thou
  Shalt find them here:

Till, as refined gold, in thee shall shine
  His image, no more dim;
Then shall the endless "afterward" be thine
  Of rest with Him.

Frances Ridley Havergal, "Afterwards," from *The Poetical Works of Frances Ridley Havergal*, 1889

Divine Purpose

Philippians 1:12-21

Philippians 1:12-21

. . . this is my prayer, that your love may overflow more and more with knowledge and full insight to help you to determine what is best, so that in the day of Christ you may be pure and blameless, having produced the harvest of righteousness that comes through Jesus Christ for the glory and praise of God.

[12]I want you to know, beloved, that what has happened to me has actually helped to spread the gospel, [13]so that it has become known throughout the whole imperial guard and to everyone else that my imprisonment is for Christ; [14]and most of the brothers and sisters, having been made confident in the Lord by my imprisonment, dare to speak the word with greater boldness and without fear.

[15]Some proclaim Christ from envy and rivalry, but others from goodwill. [16]These proclaim Christ out of love, knowing that I have been put here for the defense of the gospel; [17]the others proclaim Christ out of selfish ambition, not sincerely but intending to increase my suffering in my imprisonment. [18]What does it matter? Just this, that Christ is proclaimed in every way, whether out of false motives or true; and in that I rejoice.

Yes, and I will continue to rejoice, [19]for I know that through your prayers and the help of the Spirit of Jesus Christ this will turn out for my deliverance. [20]It is my eager expectation and hope that I will not be put to shame in any way, but that by my speaking with all boldness, Christ will be exalted now as always in my body, whether by life or by death. [21]For to me, living is Christ and dying is gain. If I am to live in the flesh, that means fruitful labor for me; and I do not know which I prefer. . . .

Scripture teaches, "The human mind may devise many plans, but it is the purpose of the Lord that will be established."[1] As we have seen, discerning God's purpose is crucial if we are going to live in God's joy. The finest Steinway piano just looks like a strange piece of furniture until the key desk is opened and the instrument is played. For us to discern God's purpose, we must be convinced that what God wills for us is the best thing that could possibly happen to us under any circumstance; we must remember that *agape* love is our primary calling; and we must be certain that the Holy Spirit will help us know God's will in any situation, revealed to us as we need it and as we are able to respond.

Paul was writing the Philippian letter from prison. Clearly imprisonment, even for the sake of the Good News, would not have been Paul's initial plan or even his choice. But that was now his circumstance. What was God's purpose? How was this the best thing that could have happened? How was imprisonment an opportunity for demonstrating *agape*?

At the core of the Good News is freedom in Jesus Christ. What an amazing opportunity: a man in chains who is preaching freedom with conviction and joy! To whom can he preach? Commentators tell us that palace guards were assigned to be with him day and night in four-hour shifts—a captive audience!

Among the Christ followers, Paul's imprisonment meant that other men and women would need to take the lead in sharing the Good News. Not only was imprisonment an opportunity for them to see the depth of Paul's belief, but it was also the catalyst for their own bold witness to be seen and heard. Maxie Dunnam has written, "We need to remember this: the fruits of our proclaiming the gospel are not only in the winning of persons to Christ, but the encouragement we give others to be bold in their Christian living and witnessing."[2]

Paul's resilient joy as he saw others strengthened by his suffering (*agape*!) will be explored further in other sections of this letter. For now, it is important to notice three sources of that joy.

First, the reason for his imprisonment was known to everyone—he had refused to renounce his faith in Jesus Christ. Because of his witness, even those who were not Christ followers were now hearing about Jesus!

Second, bold testimonies to the truth of the Good News were multiplying exponentially. Christ was being proclaimed by many different people in many different places in many different ways. While the motives of the preachers were not always pure, the Good News was being proclaimed.

Finally, Paul was eager to see what God was ultimately going to be able to accomplish in these circumstances. In prison, facing trial and possible death, Paul was almost dancing, filled with a sense of joyful urgency, eager to see whether he would have the privilege of glorifying God in a prolonged earthly life, or enjoying God in a welcomed release into eternity.

This was not the first time God had intervened in Paul's plans and changed Paul's path. At the time of his conversion, Paul was on a mission he believed was honoring God—the persecution of those who were part of The Way (Acts 9:1ff.). God stopped him. Later, Paul was determined to preach the Good News in two different regions of Asia, but he was stopped by the Holy Spirit and ended up heading in a totally different direction—that led him eventually to Philippi and the founding of this amazingly faithful congregation.

Throughout the history of the Christian faith, story after story can be found of Christ followers who sensed they were called to one ministry and found themselves redirected by God's divine purpose into a life of witness more fruitful than they could ever have expected. Again, the challenge of Ignatius Loyola is "finding God in all things in order that we might love and serve God in all things."

As we grow in discernment of God's will in any circumstance, and as the Holy Spirit reveals more to us of our unique place in God's purpose, it is possible for any Christ follower to experience such confident joy that distinctions between success or failure, acceptance or rejection, even life or death, will mean little or nothing compared to the *joy* of knowing and serving God through Jesus Christ and the power of the Holy Spirit.

For this to be our reality, we must have faith that God's will is always best in any circumstance—we cannot second-guess God. We must remember that God's purpose is always *agape* love—not the fulfillment of our perceived needs at the expense of others, but the fulfillment of others' truest needs despite the cost to us. And we must be patient as the Holy Spirit, God living in and through us, reveals God's divine purpose to us on a need-to-know and an able-to-comprehend basis.

1 Proverbs 19:21

2 Maxie D. Dunnam, *The Preacher's Commentary*, 1982

1. If you were to identify a "bold witness to Jesus Christ" among your friends and acquaintances, who comes to mind? What about this person shapes their witness?

2. How has the faith and witness of this person impacted you or changed your life?

3. How much of this person's faith is expressed verbally, and how much is communicated in other ways? In what other ways have you experienced their faith?

4. Francis of Assisi is attributed with saying, "Always preach the gospel—use words if you must." What does this say to you about proclaiming Christ in your life?

5. Have your plans and intentions ever been "redirected" by God? What was the outcome?

6. Is there a part of your life that, if God were to suddenly change it, would cause you to question God's will and God's purpose?

. . . what has happened to me has actually helped to **spread the gospel,** *. . .* **having been made confident in the Lord** *by my imprisonment, dare to speak the word with greater boldness and without fear.*

Genesis 50:20
Even though you intended to do harm to me, God intended it for good, in order to preserve a numerous people, as he is doing today.

In breaking through the chains that bind we experience a paradox—a face that shows sadness and happiness in one moment—a moment in time where we recognize that over, in, and through the chains we hold confidence in God's provisions for us.

Paul Klee, *Untitled (Trapped) / Captive (Figure of this world/next world)*, c.1940

When prison walls extend their reach
and captives are not freed,
hear us, our Father, and outstretch
your arm to meet our need.
When shadows lengthen in the days
of danger, lies and death,
grant to your church the will to pray
with clear, persistent faith.

When Christians fear that earthly
    power
will quench their liberty,
grant them the steadfast mind to know
your Word runs swift and free.
When brothers, sisters come to die
by fire or rope or gun,
grant them the grace to fix their eyes
on Christ, your risen Son.

For prison's secret miracles,
for witness borne through shame,
letters and books from lonely cells—
all glory to your name!
For converts won in high-walled yard,
for songs outlasting pain,
martyrs who gained their hope's
    reward—
our hearts give thanks again.

For love replacing cruel hate,
for enemies made friends—
Father, as all your deeds are great,
your praise shall never end.
Yours are the walls, the lock, the key,
and Christ the open door;
our justice, mercy, life and joy,
our freedom evermore.

Christopher M. Idle, *When Prison Walls Extend Their Reach*, 1993

Rachel Durfee, *For Those in Captivity*, 2002

Dearest Lord, teach us to be generous;
teach us to serve you as you deserve;
to give and not count the cost,
to fight and not heed the wounds,
to toil and not to seek for rest,
to labor and not to ask for any reward,
save that of knowing that [we] do your will.

Ignatius Loyola (1491-1556), from *2000 Years of Prayer*

We raise our eyes in prayer
through the bars, darkly.

Together with a thousand prisoners in their cells
and with many more thousands in the larger prison
of our country.

We pray for freedom
and even more urgently, for life.

As nameless executioners salvage
those whom they used to merely torture and detain
and both children and parents
slowly but surely die
of sickness that has many names
and only one name.

We ask for faith
to see that death and prison are not forever
that life and freedom will prevail.

We ask for faith
to celebrate even while we mourn
knowing that death and prison
are already signs of a people's struggle
for freedom and life.

We raise our voices in prayer
through the bars, boldly
believing there will be an answer
as our people awaken.

Amen.

Edicio de la Torre, Philippines, "Prayer for Our Times," 1984, from *Touching Ground, Taking Root*

Today hundreds of thousands of Christians live in jails and prisons throughout the world. In the United States the prison church is estimated at 165,000 members. Although the prison church has no denominational affiliation, at every opportunity brothers and sisters gather informally to speak God's Word to each other, pray together, and find comfort in recognizing Christ's presence among our fellowship. This is how we survive.

Troy Rienstra, "The Church Behind Bars," 2005

O Lord Christ,
who, when your hour was come,
went without fear
amongst those who sought your life:
grant us grace to confess you before all,
without arrogance and without fear,
that your Holy Name may be glorified.

J. H. Oldham (1874-1969), from *The Communion of Saints*

I am in Birmingham because injustice is here. Just as the prophets of the eighth century B.C. left their villages and carried their "thus saith the Lord" far beyond the boundaries of their home towns, and just as the Apostle Paul left his village of Tarsus and carried the gospel of Jesus Christ to the far corners of the Greco-Roman world, so am I compelled to carry the gospel of freedom beyond my own home town. Like Paul, I must constantly respond to the Macedonian call for aid.

Martin Luther King, Jr., "Letter from a Birmingham Jail," April 16, 1963

Steve Prince, *9 Little Indians: Letter to the Public Schools*, 2004

In these days of confused situations,
in these nights of a restless remorse,
when the heart and the soul of the nation
lay wounded and cold as a corpse,
from the grave of the innocent Adam
comes a song bringing joy to the sad.
Oh your cry has been heard and the ransom
has been paid up in full, be ye glad.

Oh, be ye glad, be ye glad.
Every debt that you ever had
has been paid up in full by the grace of the Lord.
Be ye glad, be ye glad, be ye glad.

From the dungeon a rumor is stirring.
You have heard it again and again.
But this time the cell keys are turning,
and outside there are faces of friends.

And though your body lay weary from wasting,
and your eyes show the sorrow they've had,
Oh the love that your heart is now tasting
has opened the gates, be ye glad. *Refrain*

So be like lights on the rim of the water,
giving hope in a storm sea of night.
Be a refuge amidst the slaughter
for these fugitives in their flight.
For you are timeless and part of a puzzle.
You are winsome and young as a lad.
And there is no disease or no struggle
that can pull you from God, be ye glad. *Refrain*

Michael Kelly Blanchard, *Be Ye Glad*

© See Text Sources

*Some proclaim Christ from envy and rivalry, but others from goodwill. These proclaim **Christ out of love** . . . What does it matter? Just this, that Christ is proclaimed in every way . . .*

O Lord,
let me not henceforth desire health or life
except to spend them for you, with you and in you.
You alone know what is good for me;
do therefore what seems best to you.
Give to me or take from me; conform my will to yours;
and grant that with humble and perfect submission and in holy
   confidence
I may receive the orders of your eternal providence,
and may equally adore all that comes to me from you;
through Jesus Christ our Lord.

Blaise Pascal (1623-1662), from *2000 Years of Prayer*

1 Corinthians 1:27–31

But God chose what is foolish in the world to shame the wise; God chose what is weak in the world to shame the strong; God chose what is low and despised in the world, things that are not, to reduce to nothing things that are, so that no one might boast in the presence of God. He is the source of your life in Christ Jesus, who became for us wisdom from God, and righteousness and sanctification and redemption, in order that, as it is written, "Let the one who boasts, boast in the Lord."

Sing of foolishness and wisdom,
sing the message of the cross.
By this folly we are rescued,
God's own power finding us.

Sing of those esteemed for wisdom,
who demand our minds and hearts.
God undoes their hold upon us;
at the cross our freedom starts.

Sing of those who live for power,
bending truth in grasping hands.
Truth will live and they will perish;
by a grave the victor stands.

Sing the people God has gathered;
high and low alike are here.
Some are lifted, some are humbled;
who can boast when God is near?

Sing the stumbling block, our Savior;
we will kneel before we fall.
We will rise and live with Jesus,
hear and answer God's own call.

Richard Leach, *Sing of Foolishness and Wisdom*, 2005

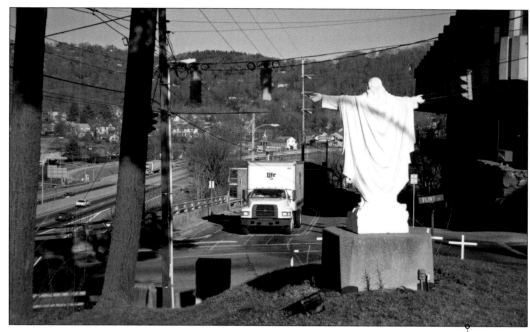

Bryan Hiott, *Divine Lite*, 1999

In Asheville, North Carolina, I encountered a concrete Jesus—a statue of the Good Shepherd, no less—on a hill across from the Civic Center, overlooking an expressway and peering through a grid of power lines toward a sadly overdeveloped mountain. This concrete Jesus, with his back to me and his arms outstretched, seemed not to be blessing the land so much as making a gesture of infinite resignation toward our poor stewardship of it. At the instant I made the photograph, a Lite Beer truck, having just emerged from a deep shadow, came to a stop before a red light at the intersection of Flint Street and Hiawassee; and this made the irony complete: out of darkness, Lite.

Bryan Hiott, 1999

Come, thou long-expected Jesus,
born to set thy people free;
from our fears and sins release us,
let us find our rest in thee.

Israel's strength and consolation,
hope of all the earth thou art:
dear desire of every nation,
joy of every longing heart.

Born thy people to deliver,
born a child and yet a king,
born to reign in us forever,
now thy gracious kingdom bring.

By thine own eternal Spirit
rule in all our hearts alone;
by thine all-sufficient merit
raise us to thy glorious throne.

Charles Wesley, *Come, Thou Long-Expected Jesus*, 1744

Ken Glaser, *Hands of Inmate on Cell Bars*

Isaiah 61:1-4

The spirit of the Lord God is upon me,
   because the Lord has anointed me;
he has sent me to bring good news to the oppressed,
   to bind up the brokenhearted,
to proclaim liberty to the captives,
   and release to the prisoners;
to proclaim the year of the Lord's favor,
   and the day of vengeance of our God;
   to comfort all who mourn;
to provide for those who mourn in Zion—
   to give them a garland instead of ashes,

the oil of gladness instead of mourning,
   the mantle of praise instead of a faint spirit.
They will be called oaks of righteousness,
   the planting of the Lord, to display his glory.
They shall build up the ancient ruins,
   they shall raise up the former devastations;
they shall repair the ruined cities,
   the devastations of many generations.

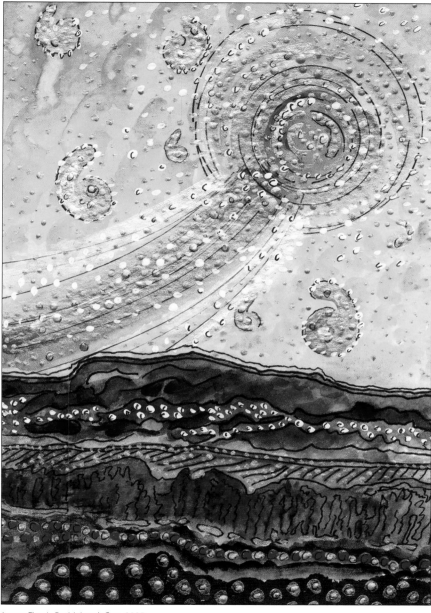

James Fissel, *Bethlehem's Star*, 2005

O bless the Lord, my soul!
Let all within me join
and help my tongue to praise his name
whose mercies are divine.

O bless the Lord, my soul!
Let not his mercies lie
forgotten in unthankfulness,
from lack of praise to die.

For God forgives our sins
and God relieves our pain;
the Lord who heals our sicknesses
renews our strength again.

His mighty works and ways
by Moses he made known,
but gave the world his truth and grace
by his beloved Son.

Isaac Watts, *O Bless the Lord, My Soul!* (after Psalm 103), 1719

*It is my **eager expectation and hope** that . . . by my speaking with all boldness, Christ will be exalted . . .*

Tim Ladwig, *Our Father in Heaven*, from *The Lord's Prayer*, 2000

Lord, bless your church, and keep us true
age after age, by trusting you.
Set our expectant hearts ablaze,
Spirit of scripture, prayer, and praise!
Gathered, we tap your vast reserve;
scattered, we take your love and serve.

Lord, bless your church, lest gain or loss
take our attention from the cross;
strengthen the hearts we lift above;
fill us with sacrificial love.
Through our communing, help us heed
calls to respond to human need.

Lord, bless your church which seeks to show
Christ in the world for all to know:
use every hand to serve as yours;
speak through each voice till truth endures.
Clothe us with love to live our creeds,
showing our faith by faithful deeds.

Lord, bless your church and dwell within—
conscience to challenge culture's sin;
rising within us, may your song
give us the will to conquer wrong.
Still be our vision, clear our view;
fill us with love and make us new!

David A. Robb, *Lord, Bless Your Church*, 1991

My Lord and my shepherd,
I have been walking in the shadow of death.
The hands of those who desire to kill me
are constantly pursuing after me.
As I face the coming crisis of death, Lord,
give me the courage to overcome the power of death.
O God, it has not been easy for me as a fragile human being
to endure the never-ending torture.
Let me persevere with the sufferings of sword and fire.
Gracious God, it is for righteousness that I live,
and it is my prayer that for righteousness I may die.
O Lord, into your hands I want to commit my spirit.
As I collapse holding the cross in my hands,
hold me in your hands and receive my spirit. Amen.

Ki-Chul Joo, Korea, tr. Eugene Eung-Chun Park, *I Will Offer My Blood* (1897-1944)

Grant me no more than to be a sacrifice for God
while there is an altar at hand. Then you can form
yourselves into a choir and sing praises to the Father
in Jesus Christ that God gave the bishop of Syria
the privilege of reaching the sun's setting when he
summoned him from its rising. It is a grand thing for
my life to set on the world, and for me to be on my
way to God, so that I may rise in his presence.

Ignatius, *The Letters of Ignatius, Bishop of Antioch: To the Romans*, c. A.D. 100

In life or death, Lord Jesus Christ,
be all in all, I pray;
your life, your death make known in me
on earth, till heaven's day.

In sun or shadow be my help;
your voice shall guide my feet:
teach me by your incisive word;
your work in me complete.
In calm or crisis, be my hope
and take my mind in hand;
so shall I trust you, even where
I cannot understand.

In loss or profit, be my joy;
my hours for you be spent:
I can do all things in your strength;
so shall I be content.

In risk or safety, be my friend;
I place my hand in yours,
with you to rest, or wait, or walk,
or run with all my powers.

O Christ, my help, my hope, my joy,
my all-enduring Friend,
all that I am belongs to you
who loved me to the end.

Christopher M. Idle, *In Life or Death, Lord Jesus Christ*,
1993

Bagong Kussudiardja, *The Ascension*, 1984

Standing Firm

Philippians 1:22-30

Philippians 1:22-30

. . . For to me, living is Christ and dying is gain. [22]If I am to live in the flesh, that means fruitful labor for me; and I do not know which I prefer. [23]I am hard pressed between the two: my desire is to depart and be with Christ, for that is far better; [24]but to remain in the flesh is more necessary for you. [25]Since I am convinced of this, I know that I will remain and continue with all of you for your progress and joy in faith, [26]so that I may share abundantly in your boasting in Christ Jesus when I come to you again.

[27]Only, live your life in a manner worthy of the gospel of Christ, so that, whether I come and see you or am absent and hear about you, I will know that you are standing firm in one spirit, striving side by side with one mind for the faith of the gospel, [28]and are in no way intimidated by your opponents. For them this is evidence of their destruction, but of your salvation. And this is God's doing. [29]For he has graciously granted you the privilege not only of believing in Christ, but of suffering for him as well— [30]since you are having the same struggle that you saw I had and now hear that I still have.

If then there is any encouragement in Christ, any consolation from love, any sharing in the Spirit, any compassion and sympathy, make my joy complete . . .

Suffering for Jesus is only a concept for many people who will read this book. We in the post-modern West live in a culture that values tolerance over conviction. As long as Christ followers remain passive about faith, especially about witnessing to the reality of ultimate truth, the particular details of personal piety will, for the most part, remain unquestioned by the culture and the keepers of its norms. Honoring this form of cultural condescension seems to be the ultimate goal of many contemporary people, even in the Church.

Relativism, the theory that one set of beliefs is as good as any other, combined with "polite" practices of faith at the expense of core convictions, is nothing new. The Good News that Jesus Christ is *the* way, *the* truth, *the* life, and *the only* access we have to God, has threatened many cultures and governments. Christ followers who choose to not keep the Good News contained suffer.

Paul was imprisoned because he refused to stay in that cultural box. God had ambushed Paul on the Damascus Road, annihilating his dependence on everything he once cherished, including the approval of his native culture. He now proclaimed Jesus Christ with even more zeal than he had, years earlier, for exposing and expunging the witness of other Christ followers.

Even for Paul, however, the experience of the power of Christ, the recognition that God has begun a good work in us, is only the beginning, never an end in itself. Paul's encounter on the Damascus Road, his boldness in witness, his determination to preach Christ in the synagogues of the Jews and the academies of the Gentiles, could simply have been a trophy both for him and for the rank and file in Philippi—the epic legend of their infamous founder. In reality, Paul's legendary zeal, his unquenchable joy, his determination to share Christ in every circumstance were only markers used by the Holy Spirit to reveal God's greater purpose to the Philippian congregation of converts, affirming that the Good News was real.

That was the first part of his message. As he was writing, Paul was suffering—so what? Earthly suffering could never take away the joy of glorifying God. Even the momentary inconvenience of imprisonment could not diminish the transcendent joy he had found in Jesus Christ.

Paul was living life large, even in chains. For him, life itself was a witness to Christ, and death was only an improvement. His was a life few have ever known, with a level of spiritual freedom, grace, peace and joy few have ever experienced and even fewer have ever tried to express. In this opening part of the Philippian letter, we hear the joy-cry of a human heart truly at worship: "Hear my praise, loving Lord—the unrestrained, unbridled, uninhibited joy I have found in you alone. I'll keep on worshiping you here—undistracted, undiminished, and undeterred, no matter what the circumstances of my life may be, until you bring me home!"

Human beings are experiential creatures, yet in many ways, we insulate our lives, keeping our experience of Christ's transformation limited. The shallow claims and seductions of the world seem much more real and irresistible. As a result, many Christ followers don't have a clue how numb we really are, how shallow our prayers have become, and how anemic and lame our expressions in worship sound in comparison with Spirit-inspired praise.

We have never known God's freedom—full release from anxiety, guilt, and the need for continuous acknowledgement, acceptance, and emotional self-service. The power of the Good News is diminished in us. The promises of God are more like a marinade than the meat of our lives. We can attempt a life of faith, or not, depending on our appetites each day. We do not value Christ enough to be inconvenienced by him for very long.

Paul must have found among the Philippian Christ followers an uncommon commitment to the Good News. He was honest with them about his suffering, but also about the reality that they themselves had been gifted (v. 29) not only with the depth of grace to believe in Christ, but also with the strength of grace to endure suffering for Christ. They were suffering even as they were listening to his words. If they were faithful, they could only expect suffering to increase. Christ followers suffer, but suffering only brings a deeper experience of

faith. God who began this good work would be faithful. The question is, would they—will we?

Forbid it, Lord, that I should boast
save in the death of Christ my God;
all the vain things that charm me most,
I sacrifice them to his blood.

His dying crimson like a robe
spreads o'er his body on the Tree;
then am I dead to all the globe,
and all the globe is dead to me.

Were the whole realm of nature mine,
that were a present far too small;
Love, so amazing, so divine,
demands my soul, my life, my all. [1]

1 Isaac Watts, *When I Survey the Wondrous Cross*, 1707

1. *Has there been a time when you endured suffering because of your beliefs or convictions? What form did that suffering take? Reflect on that time and what you learned from it.*

2. *How is Jesus Christ depicted in your culture? Is he the same Jesus you see in Scripture?*

3. *How accurately does your experience of church—fellowship, worship, teaching, outreach, mission—reflect Jesus Christ as you see him in Scripture?*

4. *In what ways do you find yourself or your congregation trying to make Jesus Christ and the Good News conform to the expectations of your culture?*

5. *What about Jesus Christ is so important to you that you would be willing to suffer and even die rather than renounce him?*

6. *Read some accounts of contemporary people who are suffering because they are Christ followers. How does their story speak to you? How is their story part of yours?*

If I am to live in the flesh, that means fruitful labor for me . . .

Jean-François Millet, *The Angelus*, 1857

So then, we do good works, but not for merit—for what would we merit? Rather, we are indebted to God for the good works we do, and not he to us, since it is he who "works in us both to will and do according to his good pleasure" . . . *(Phil. 2:13).*

The Belgic Confession, 1561

God, bless your church
    with strength!
    Wherever we may be,
build up your servants as
    we work in common
    ministry.
Urge us from fledgling
    faith to venture and to
    soar
through open skies,
    to sing the praise of
    Christ, whom we
    adore.

God, bless your church
    with life! May all our
    branches thrive
unblemished, wholesome,
    bearing fruit,
    abundantly alive.
From you, one Holy Vine,
    in freedom may we
    grow.
Sustain us in our
    mission, Lord, your
    love and peace to show.

God, bless your church
    with hope! Despite
    chaotic days,
may we in darkness shine
    to light a pathway
    through life's maze.
May justice be our aim,
    and kindness ours to
    share,
in humbleness O may we
    walk, assured our God
    is there. Amen.

John A. Dalles, *God, Bless Your
Church with Strength!,* 1984

Come, Holy Spirit, come! Inflame our souls with love,
transforming ev'ry heart and home with wisdom from above.
O let us not despise the humble path Christ trod,
but choose, to shame the worldly-wise, the foolishness of God.

All-knowing Spirit, prove the poverty of pride,
by knowledge of the Father's love in Jesus crucified.
And grant us faith to know the glory of that sign,
and in our very lives to show the marks of love divine.

Come with the gift to heal the wounds of guilt and fear,
and to oppression's face reveal the kingdom drawing near.
Where chaos longs to reign, descend, O holy Dove,
and free us all to work again the miracles of love.

Spirit of truth, arise; inspire the prophet's voice:
expose to scorn the tyrant's lies, and bid the poor rejoice.
O Spirit, clear our sight, all prejudice remove,
and help us to discern the right, and covet only love.

Give us the tongues to speak, in ev'ry time and place,
to rich, to poor, to strong and weak, the word of love and grace.
Enable us to hear the words that others bring,
interpreting with open ear the special song they sing.

Come, Holy Spirit, dance within our hearts today,
our earthbound spirit to entrance, our mortal fears allay.
And teach us to desire, all other things above,
that self-consuming holy fire, the perfect gift of love!

Michael Forster, *Come, Holy Spirit, Come*, 1992

Edicio de la Torre, *Kalayaan (Freedom),* 1979

Only, live your life in a manner worthy of the gospel of Christ, so that . . . I will know that you are standing firm in one spirit, striving side by side with one mind . . .

Guide us, O Lord, in all the changes and varieties of the world;
that we may have evenness and tranquility of spirit:
that we may not murmur in adversity nor in prosperity wax proud,
but in serene faith resign our souls to thy divinest will;
through Jesus Christ our Lord.

Jeremy Taylor (1613-1667), from *2000 Years of Prayer*

Lord God of heaven,
you are great and we stand in awe of you.
You faithfully keep your new covenant
with those people who trust in you and in Jesus
    Christ,
whom you have sent.
Look down on us, Lord,
and hear our prayers
as we pray for your Church here in this nation.
We confess that we, your people, have sinned.
We and all the people of this nation
have gone away from you and your Gospel,
the Good News about Jesus Christ.

Remember now what you have done in him
and not what we deserve.
For his sake renew and restore your people,
rebuild your Church and win this nation
for Christ and his Gospel once again.

We ask this in his name and for your honor and glory.

Crosswinds, England, from *Prayers Encircling the World*, 1998

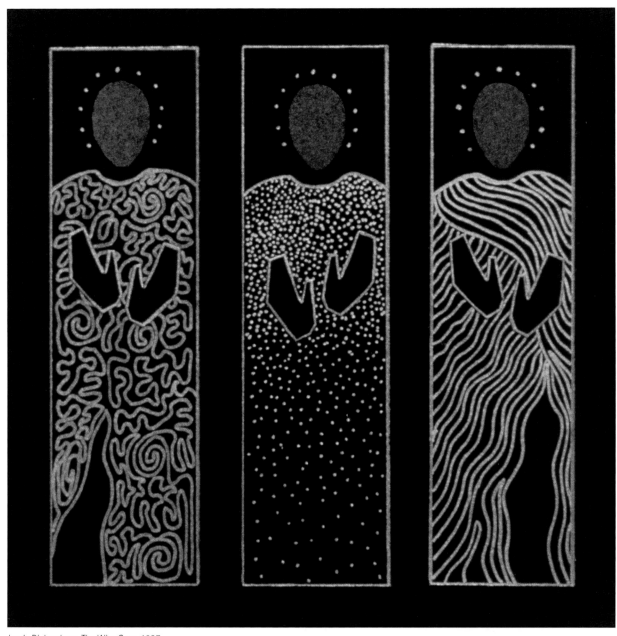

Jan L. Richardson, *The Wise Ones*, 1997

Magrit Prigge, *Fiery Furnace*, 2002

This is my one, my lifelong wish:
that I should serve the Lord,
that the day I depart this world,
I'll see God face to face.

Though we face many fiery trials,
let us not be afraid;
for with the power of Jesus Christ,
we'll overcome them all.

More precious than gold is faith,
treasure that lasts for life;
all who believe this truth are blest,
finding abundant joy.

Time like an arrow swiftly flies;
let's use our time for him.
With all our hearts and minds and
    strength,
let's labor for our Lord.

Anonymous, Korea; para. Marion Kim, *This Is My One, My Lifelong Wish / Nae pyŏngsaeng sowŏn*

God the Creator,
Thou hast changed us.
Christ the Redeemer,
Thou hast changed us.
Holy Spirit, the Binder,
Thou dost keep us changed:
Even as our lives are bound together
    in Thee.

George F. MacLeod, excerpt, "An Earth Redeemed," from *The Whole Earth Shall Cry Glory*, 2007

Finding One Mind

Philippians 2:1-4

Philippians 2:1-4

. . . For he has graciously granted you the privilege not only of believing in Christ, but of suffering for him as well— since you are having the same struggle that you saw I had and now hear that I still have.

[1]If then there is any encouragement in Christ, any consolation from love, any sharing in the Spirit, any compassion and sympathy, [2]make my joy complete: be of the same mind, having the same love, being in full accord and of one mind. [3]Do nothing from selfish ambition or conceit, but in humility regard others as better than yourselves. [4]Let each of you look not to your own interests, but to the interests of others. Let the same mind be in you that was in Christ Jesus . . .

Dietrich Bonhoeffer wrote, "Cheap grace is the deadly enemy of our Church. . . . grace as a doctrine, a principle, a system. It means forgiveness of sins proclaimed as a general truth, the love of God taught as the Christian 'conception' of God."[1] Bonhoeffer was inviting Christ followers to rediscover true (costly) discipleship amid a world of jealousy, greed, envy, and hatred, and within a church that had forgotten its first love—Jesus Christ.

Nineteen centuries earlier, the Apostle Paul warned against cheap unity—the deadly enemy of Christian identity and mission. Cheap unity is a form of free association around a slogan or an ideology among people who claim identity with Christ, even community under the name of Christ, but without the personal sacrifice required for Christ-like living. Cheap unity finds no need for the surrender of personal will to the will of God, for giving without expecting anything in return, for true *agape*—loving concern for others that eclipses preoccupation with self.

Tod Bolsinger has written:

The love shared in the Trinity and brought into the world by Jesus is the very same merciful and gracious love that is meant to be shared, demonstrated, and offered to others in and through the church. To believe in the Trinity is to live the Trinity. To live the Trinity is to be part of God's relational-sacramental life.[2]

Nothing was more important to Paul than the Good News—the transformation of the world the resurrection of Jesus Christ had begun. Flogging, imprisonment, shipwreck, even the threat of imminent death could not pull him off message. But even Christ followers who know the truth of the Resurrection struggle when they try to live together in selfless humility. Every congregation struggles with single-minded unity in Christ.

To Christ followers in Corinth Paul wrote,

. . . If anyone is in Christ, there is a new creation: everything old has passed away; see, everything has become new! All this is from God, who reconciled us to himself through Christ, and has given us the ministry of reconciliation. . . .[3]

To the congregation in Rome Paul wrote,

I appeal to you therefore, brothers and sisters, by the mercies of God, to present your bodies as a living sacrifice, holy and acceptable to God, which is your spiritual worship. Do not be conformed to this world, but be transformed by the renewing of your minds, so that you may discern what is the will of God— what is good and acceptable and perfect.[4]

And, to Ephesian believers Paul wrote,

You were taught to put away your former way of life, your old self, corrupt and deluded by its lusts, and to be renewed in the spirit of your minds, and to clothe yourselves with the new self, created according to the likeness of God in true righteousness and holiness.[5]

Paul knew that the Christ followers in Philippi had experienced the blessing of God's costly grace. Christ was their joy! Now they must deepen the focus of their life, their work, their prayer, their love, their ambition— finding their unity of identity in Christ alone.

A church divided against itself cannot stand (Matthew 12:25). But a church united by anything less than the word and the witness of Jesus Christ won't stand long. John Calvin wrote, ". . . apart from the Lord's Word there is not an agreement of believers but a faction of wicked [people] . . . whenever church unity is commended to us, this is required: that while our minds agree in Christ, our wills should also be joined with mutual benevolence in Christ."[6]

Watchman Nee told of a believer who was a rice farmer. Every morning he would pump water into his rice fields. Every night, his fields would be dry because a neighbor had opened the levies between their fields and all his water was nourishing the neighbor's crops. The farmer tried to ignore the problem but he could not. After he prayed with fellow believers, he devised a plan. One morning he filled the neighbor's fields first and then he filled his own. The neighbor, overcome by the humility of this Christian farmer, became a believer himself.

Unity in Christ's humility does not come easily. C. S. Lewis wrote, "If anyone would like to acquire humility, I can, I think, tell him the first step. The first step is to realize that one is proud. [This is] a biggish step too. At least, nothing whatever can be done before it."[7]

Many influential Christian leaders and vibrant Christian mission efforts have been undermined by petty rivalry, jealousy, the desire for power, or the need to be "right." Christ followers bicker and divide over issues that pale in comparison to the opportunity of proclaiming Christ amid an unbelieving world. The gospel suffers. The Holy Spirit can transform our meager attempts at cheap unity into a devoted covenant fellowship—vibrant in our proclamation, united in mind and in purpose: a transformed community of God's amazing grace. But this transformation cannot begin until we surrender ourselves to the selfless Self and become single-minded within the mind of Christ.

1 Dietrich Bonhoeffer, *The Cost of Discipleship*, 1959

2 Tod E. Bolsinger, *It Takes a Church to Raise a Christian*, 2004

3 2 Corinthians 5:17-18

4 Romans 12:1-2

5 Ephesians 4:22-24

6 John Calvin, *Institutes of the Christian Religion*, 1536

7 C. S. Lewis, *Mere Christianity*, 1952

1. *Ask several people in your congregation to complete this sentence: "In our congregation, we are all _____." What is uniting them?*

2. *What do "cheap grace" and "cheap unity" require of an individual? What is the outcome of cheap grace and cheap unity for a congregation?*

3. *God's saving grace is costly—our freedom from sin was bought at a price (1 Corinthians 6–7). Reread the excerpts from Scripture included in this chapter. How costly is "unity with the mind of Christ" for you or your congregation?*

4. *How does "unity with the mind of Christ" promote God's shalom?*

5. *How does "unity with the mind of Christ" inspire expressions of agape?*

6. *What part of your life is most difficult to surrender for the sake of unity with the mind of Christ?*

***If then there is** any encouragement in Christ, **any consolation** from love, **any sharing** in the Spirit, **any compassion and sympathy** . . .*

1 Corinthians 12:4-6
Now there are varieties of gifts, but the same Spirit; and there are varieties of services, but the same Lord; and there are varieties of activities, but it is the same God who activates all of them in everyone.

Romans 12:5
. . . we, who are many, are one body in Christ, and individually we are members one of another.

In recalling their life as a community formed by the gospel, Paul uses [here] a number of the key words from chapter one: joy, fellowship, love, partnership, affection, unity, and mindset or attitude, . . . and he does so in language that assumes these experiences are already genuinely theirs.

Fred B. Craddock, *Philippians*, 1985

Joseph O'Connell, *Community*, 1985

Leonard Freed, *Return of Martin Luther King Jr., after receiving Nobel Peace Prize*, Baltimore, 1963 (photo detail)

Called to be servants, called to be sons,
called to be daughters, we're called to be one.
Called into service, called to be free;
you are called to be you, and I'm called to be me.

Children, come with wide open eyes.
Look at the water; you have been baptized.
You're free from the slav'ry that bound you to sin,
so live now as children in the kingdom of heav'n.
Refrain

We are saints! Forgiveness is sure,
not of ourselves, but the cross Christ endured.
We're free from the law that said "You must provide!"
We're free to be servants; we're called, we're baptized.
Refrain

Jesus closed the dark pit of death.
He has breathed on us with his holy breath.
He gives us the faith to respond to his News.
We're free to show mercy, to love, to be bruised.
Refrain

James G. Johnson, *Called to Be Servants*

Jesus as the great leader of the sheep. The church as those who strive to be led by Jesus. [That doesn't] always match our experience as the church. We wouldn't have to work very hard, preacher and congregation, to remind ourselves of those times in church history, those times in the church's life, those times in a congregation when someone had to push and prod and even shout, when church life looks a lot more like herding cats, when new ideas drop like lead balloons, when a prophet's voice for justice is squelched by those who equate the status quo and the preservation of power and just plain nostalgia with the gospel itself. . . .

David A. Davis, "The Shepherd's Voice," 2006

. . . make my joy complete . . .

John August Swanson, *Celebration*, 1997

© 1997 by John August Swanson

Come celebrate the journey
begun so long ago:
A Church, formed by the Spirit,
God's love and peace to show,
was faithfully assembled
together in one place,
to worship, work and witness,
united by Christ's grace.

John A. Dalles, *Come Celebrate the Journey* (stanza 1),
1987

Elizabeth Steele Halstead, *The Heavens and the Earth*, 1985

Come celebrate the journey,
the pathway now is ours,
to find, to blaze, to follow
as God grants and empow'rs;
the Spirit's calling beckons
through all earth's breadth and length,
with words of exultation:
"Move on, from strength to strength!"

John A. Dalles, *Come Celebrate the Journey* (stanza 2), 1987

Come celebrate the journey
God's vision to behold.
Come, spread the Gospel message,
God's future to enfold.
How blessed are the people
who heed God's joyful sound,
for they shall live in glory,
and in God's light, abound!

John A. Dalles, *Come Celebrate the Journey* (stanza 3), 1987

Emil Nolde, *Wildtanzende Kinder (Wildly Dancing Children)*, 1909

. . . be of the same mind, *having the same love, being in full accord and of one mind.*

Paul Stoub, *Children of the Light*, 1973

Psalm 133
How good and pleasant it is
    when God's people live together in unity!

It is like precious oil poured on the head,
    running down on the beard,
    running down on Aaron's beard,
    down on the collar of his robe.

It is as if the dew of Hermon
    were falling on Mount Zion.
    For there the Lord bestows his blessing,
    even life forevermore. *TNIV*

O God, who hast bound us together in this bundle of life; give us grace to understand how our lives depend upon the courage, the industry, the honesty and the integrity of our fellow-men; that we may be mindful of their needs, grateful for their faithfulness, and faithful in our responsibilities to them; through Jesus Christ our Lord.

Reinhold Niebuhr, *Hymns for Worship*, 1939

Saint Hildegard von Bingen (1098–1179), *"All creation praises the Lord,"* the nine choirs of the angels, from *Liber Scivias (Know the ways of the Lord)*

Dinah Roe Kendall, *Jesus Washing the Disciples' Feet*, 1996

Ephesians 3:20-21
Now to him who by the power at work within us is able to accomplish abundantly far more than all we can ask or imagine, to him be glory in the church and in Christ Jesus to all generations, forever and ever. Amen.

O LORD Jesus Christ,
Thou didst not come to the world to be served,
but also surely not to be admired
or in that sense to be worshiped.
Thou wast the way and the truth—
and it was followers only Thou didst demand.
Arouse us therefore
if we have dozed away into this delusion,
save us from the error of wishing to admire Thee
instead of being willing to follow Thee
and to resemble Thee.

Søren Kierkegaard (1813–1855), *Training in Christianity*

I do not give you orders as if I were
somebody important. For even if I am
a prisoner for the Name, I have not
yet reached Christian perfection. I am
only beginning to be a disciple, so I
address you as my fellow students.
I needed your coaching in faith,
encouragement, endurance, and
patience.

Ignatius, *The Letters of Ignatius, Bishop of Antioch: To the
Ephesians*, c. A.D. 100

Lord, help us walk your servant way
wherever love may lead
and, bending low, forgetting self,
each serve the other's need.

You came to earth, O Christ, as Lord,
but pow'r you laid aside.
You lived your years in servanthood,
in lowliness you died.

No golden scepter but a towel
you place within the hands
of those who seek to follow you
and live by your commands.

You bid us bend our human pride
nor count ourselves above
the lowest place, the meanest task
that waits the gift of love.

Lord, help us walk your servant way
wherever love may lead
and, bending low, forgetting self,
each serve the other's need.

Herman G. Stuempfle, Jr., *Lord, Help Us Walk Your
Servant Way*, 1994

Imitating Christ

Philippians 2:5-11

Philippians 2:5-11

[5]Let the same mind be in you that was in Christ Jesus,

[6]who, though he was in the form of God,
did not regard equality with God
as something to be exploited,
[7]but emptied himself,
taking the form of a slave,
being born in human likeness.
And being found in human form,
[8]he humbled himself
and became obedient to the point of death—
even death on a cross.

[9]Therefore God also highly exalted him
and gave him the name
that is above every name,
[10]so that at the name of Jesus
every knee should bend,
in heaven and on earth and under the earth,
[11]and every tongue should confess
that Jesus Christ is Lord,
to the glory of God the Father.

On the previous page, you encountered a holy and beautiful text—a hymn of praise to Christ the Redeemer from an impassioned convert; a confident witness to God's love from a forgiven sinner; a case for the centrality of the Cross from the greatest theological mind of the first century; an outburst of joy from a devoted disciple—all in six short verses!

Earl Palmer has written that in this passage Paul gives "the ultimate example . . . the only life ever lived with full and final integrity."[1] James Boice said, "This passage is among the most glorious sections of the New Testament. In these few verses we see the great sweep of Christ's life from eternity past to eternity future. And we are admitted to the breathtaking purposes of God. . . ."[2]

Human beings are more sinful than we can ever imagine, and in Jesus Christ we are more loved than we can ever know. This reality falls hard on the ears of contemporary Western people. Post-modern Christ followers are inoculated to the power of this Good News by a culture of aggressive indifference. We have no problem believing our lives are flawed and incomplete, and that somehow we were created for something more. What we cannot seem to understand is that "more" is gained only from honest humility—emptying ourselves of all we have earned and our assumptions about all we deserve. A generation ago, Carl Jung told the story of a man who asked a rabbi why, in the time of the Bible, God would reveal himself to many people, but recently no one ever sees him. "Why is this," the man wanted to know. The rabbi answered, "Because nowadays no one bows low enough."

Human pride is nothing new. People of every generation look for heroes to imitate. To Paul's Gentile peers, men like Alexander the Great and his father Philip II (for whom the city of Philippi was named) were gods. Monuments were built to honor these great men. The Good News of salvation through the literal humiliation of God offended the Gentiles as well as the Jews. As N. T. Wright has observed, "[People] . . . were shocked beyond belief at the idea that the one true God might be known at last in the person of a crucified Jew."[3] Paul's Philippian hymn was not intended to function like a Greco-Roman statue, or as a tribute by one Jew to honor another. In these verses Paul simply expresses the honest joy he experiences whenever he thinks about Jesus.

Many people can take this Good News for granted, much like walking past a war monument with only a fleeting glance. Even in the times set aside for "worship," we can sing hymns, hear testimonies of personal transformation, and return to life as usual, unimpressed by the glory of God's sacrifice, uninspired to change our habits, or reorganize our priorities, or redirect the trajectory of our lives.

Charles Wesley got it. He understood the message of Paul's Philippian hymn. Around the time of his personal conversion to belief in Jesus Christ, Wesley wrote his own hymn, based on Paul's letters to Philippi and Rome and passages from the Acts of the Apostles. Wesley's refrain summarizes the poem, "*Amazing* love! How can it be that *you*, my *Lord*, should *die* for *me*?"[4] (emphasis added).

God set aside all the glory and honor he was due to accomplish his purpose in Jesus Christ: "emptied himself," as Wesley wrote, ". . . of all but [his] love." And love is all God needed to redeem his children and begin to restore his sin-vandalized world. Undistracted by sin and impervious to the lies of the Enemy, God-in-the-flesh could feed multitudes, heal the sick, even raise the dead without breaking a sweat. These events are not miracles. In God's presence, people don't starve, or suffer, or die. The miracle was God, willing to move into our world, to show us the extent of his power and the intent of his love.

Paul initially invited the Philippian Christ followers to be like-minded—experiencing the same love from God, being one in God's Spirit and one in God's purpose. Now his challenge was to be united in determination to live in honest humility, emptied of all claim to personal honor, status, and self-importance, serving one another and serving the non-believing world with sincere humility and with sacrificial love.

The story has been told about a village in Africa in which there were two hospitals: the missionary hospital, a government hospital adjacent to it, and then the village beyond. Yet the village people routinely walked past the government hospital to receive care from the staff of the missionary hospital. This seemed strange since both facilities dispensed the same medicine. When asked why they did this, village people responded, "The medicine may be the same, but the hands dispensing it are different." In this great and beautiful hymn, Paul challenges us to imitate the Servant-God, dispensing Good News with humility and living Good News with love.

1 Earl F. Palmer, *Integrity*, 2000

2 James Montgomery Boice, *Philippians*, 1971

3 Tom Wright, *Paul for Everyone*, 2004

4 Charles Wesley, *And Can It Be*, 1738

1. *Carefully reread Philippians 2:5–11. What difference does Paul suggest the humiliation and exaltation of Jesus can make in your life?*

2. *Some people argue that if Jesus Christ was truly God, there are things about him no mere human should be expected to imitate. How would Paul respond? How would you respond?*

3. *If you began to "empty yourself of all but love," what would be some of the first things that would have to go? What would be the hardest things for you to release?*

4. *Do you think it would be easier to express true humility in your life if people closest to you were attempting to live this way as well? Why? What does this tell you about communities of Christ followers?*

5. *What does it mean to you that Jesus needed to die to free you from the power of sin? What does it mean to you that Jesus gladly did this? What specific difference does this belief make in your daily life?*

6. *What other "gods" compete with Jesus Christ in your life? What could help you reject these "little gods" and be more completely focused on Jesus Christ as your one and only Lord?*

Let the same mind be in you *that was in Christ Jesus . . .*

Rick Beerhorst, *The Imitation of Christ*, 2005

Lord, strip my righteousness away
and dress me in your grace,
for I cannot endure my pride
while looking at your face.

For when I look upon your face,
I feel unclothed and bare.
I know that I am dressed in rags
and need a robe to wear.

The shining robe I need to wear
to stand before your throne
is woven from the seamless love
that took me as your own.

In death you took me as your own;
your rising set me free,
when you gave up your righteousness
to dress and cover me.

Gracia Grindal, *The Joyful Exchange*, 2005

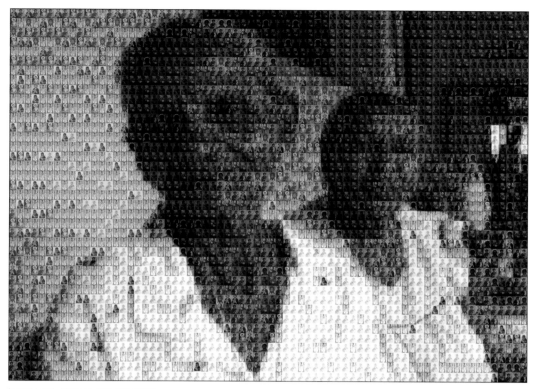

Laurel Lozzi, *Mary and Martha*, 2006

Holy Spirit,
think through me
till your ideas are my
ideas.

attr. Amy Carmichael (1867-1951)

. . . who . . . **emptied himself**, *taking the form of a slave, being born in human likeness.*
And being found in human form, he humbled himself . . .

One with God before creation,
bringing stars and suns to birth.
Christ, you cast aside your glory;
as a servant walked the earth.

> *Let your mind, O Christ, be in us,*
> *forming us in all our ways.*
> *Let your light and love surround us,*
> *guarding, guiding all our days.*

Emptied now of gain and glory,
one with our humanity,
all our pain and grief embracing
by your love so full and free.

Source of life, all life sustaining,
giver of the Spirit's breath,
yet upon the cross you suffered,
faithful even unto death.

God has raised you up in triumph
over death's defiant claim.
Help us sing with awe your praises;
may our tongues confess your name.

Jesus Christ! Your name in splendor
dims the light of star and sun!
May the church proclaim your glory
while the centuries onward run!

Herman G. Stuempfle, Jr., *One with God before Creation*,
1997

Sandra Bowden, *In the Beginning
Was the Word*, 1982

Anonymous, *Christ with the Crown of Thorns*, 20th century

O sacred head, now wounded,
with grief and shame weighed down,
now scornfully surrounded
with thorns, your only crown.
O sacred head, what glory
and blessing you have known!
Yet, though despised and gory,
I claim you as my own.

My Lord, what you did suffer
was all for sinners' gain;
mine, mine was the transgression,
but yours the deadly pain.
So here I kneel, my Savior,
for I deserve your place;
look on me with your favor
and save me by your grace.

What language shall I borrow
to thank you, dearest Friend,
for this, your dying sorrow,
your mercy without end?
Lord, make me yours forever,
a loyal servant true,
and let me never,
never outlive my love for you.

Bernard of Clairvaux, *O Sacred Head, Now Wounded*, 12th century

It is some anonymous African craftsman carving a face only a few inches high . . . who tells us that a god who would so demean himself, if there is such a god, is the only god worth living and dying for. It is the face of Christ crowned with thorns, a black Christ carved on a book end out of some dark wood that has been sanded and mellowed to a soft sheen. . . . There is no way of saying all that shines out of such a face other than the way the wood has said it. Compassion, beauty, sorrow, majesty, love—

— Frederick Buechner, *The Faces of Jesus*, 1974

Bruce Herman, *The Crowning*, 1991

O love, how deep, how broad, how
   high,
how passing thought and fantasy,
that God, the Son of God, should take
our mortal form for mortals' sake!

For us baptized, for us he bore
his holy fast and hungered sore,
for us temptation sharp he knew;
for us the tempter overthrew.

For us he prayed; for us he taught;
for us his daily works he wrought;
by words and signs and actions thus
still seeking not himself, but us.

For us to evil pow'rs betrayed,
scourged, mocked, in purple robe
   arrayed,
he bore the shameful cross and death,
for us gave up his dying breath.

For us he rose from death again;
for us he went on high to reign;
for us he sent his Spirit here,
to guide, to strengthen and to cheer.

All glory to our Lord and God
for love so deep, so high, so broad:
the Trinity, whom we adore
forever and forevermore.

Thomas à Kempis, *O Love, How Deep, How Broad, How High*, 15th century

88

Henri Matisse, *Icarus*, plate VIII from the illustrated book "Jazz," 1947

Marc Chagall, *White Crucifixion*, 1938

Marc Chagall, French, born Vitebsk, Russia (present-day Belarus), 1887-1985, White Crucifixion, 1938, Oil on canvas, 154.3 x 139.7 cm, Gift of Alfred S. Alschuler, 1946.925, The Art Institute of Chicago. Photography © The Art Institute of Chicago. © 2009 Artists Rights Society (ARS), New York / ADAGP, Paris.

Holy God,
Holy and mighty,
Holy immortal One, have mercy upon us.

My peace I gave, which the world cannot give,
and washed your feet as a sign of my love,
but you draw the sword to strike in my name
and seek high places in my kingdom.
I offered you my body and blood,
but you scatter and deny and abandon me,
and you have prepared a cross for your Savior.

Trisagion, ancient hymn; Solemn Reproaches of the Cross, 9th–11th centuries

Chagall's Christ seems to float weightlessly in front of the cross at the center of a world in chaos.

At the upper left, and reading counterclockwise, we see a threatening mob carrying flags and brandishing weapons, an overturned house and homes aflame, . . . three persons huddled despondently together, for the boat in which the villagers flee has left without them. In the lower left foreground an old man weeps as he disappears from view. . . . At the foot of the cross a ceremonial branched candlestick burns serenely, . . . an anguished mother hurries forward pressing her infant's head against her own cheek. An old peasant with a sack on his back flees amid the flames which seem to issue from the open scroll. . . . In the upper right, a synagogue is aflame . . . meeting the shaft of white light which cuts diagonally down across the scene, surrounding the crucified Christ and focusing our attention on his figure. The structure of the painting is made up of many diagonal movements, the skewed tau-shaped cross proclaiming the central thrusts. The shaft of light and the pyramidal hill . . . are opposed by the diagonals of the fleeing figures . . . accentuating the dissonance and unresolved chaotic movement of the composition.

The focal point of the whole composition is the round nimbus of light behind the head of Christ. This disc of light is repeated in the glow about the candelabra . . . [above the cross] four figures . . . gesture sorrowfully, three of them in the ancient pantomime: see no evil, hear no evil, speak no evil.

Jane Dillenberger, *Secular Art with Sacred Themes*, 1969

90

Mathias Gruenewald, *Crucifixion*. A panel from the Isenheim Altar, c.1515

And can it be that I should gain
an interest in the Savior's blood?
Died he for me, who caused his pain—
for me, who caused his bitter death?
Amazing love! How can it be
that you, my Lord, should die for me?

   Amazing love! How can it be
   that you, my Lord, should die for me?

He left his Father's throne above—
so free, so infinite his grace—
emptied himself of all but love,
and bled for Adam's helpless race!
What mercy this, immense and free,
for, O my God, it found out me!

Long my imprisoned spirit lay
fast bound in sin and nature's night.
Your sunrise turned that night to day;
I woke—the dungeon flamed with light!
My chains fell off, your voice I knew;
I rose, went out, and followed you.

No condemnation now I dread,
for Christ, and all in him, is mine!
Alive in him, my living Head,
and clothed in righteousness divine,
bold I approach th'eternal throne
and claim the crown, through Christ,
   my own.

Charles Wesley, *And Can It Be*, 1738

Pablo Picasso, *The Crucifixion*, 1930

It is the smiling face on Christ's left that stays with me, however, almost like an emblem: those dark red glasses providing incognito status and the stupid, self-satisfied smile of spectators who look on suffering with hypocritical interest, totally unmoved to enter into the trouble. This painting depicts a world seriously out of joint; it exaggerates the savage agony and comfortable smirks which constitute the aftermath of the crucifixion.

Calvin Seerveld, *Bearing Fresh Olive Leaves*, 2000

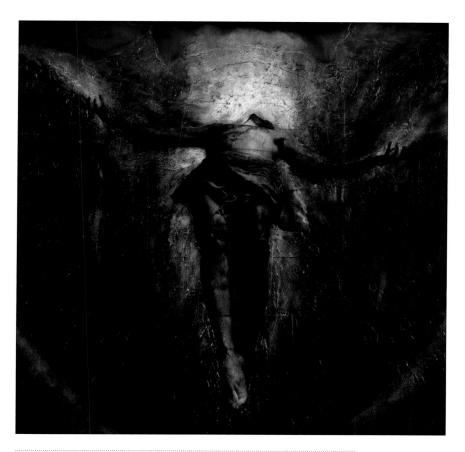

Kevin Rolly, *Forsaken (The Crucifixion)*, 2005

. . . The circle of our understanding
Is a very restricted area. . . .
What is happening outside of the circle?
And what is the meaning of happening? . . .
And what is being done to us?
And what are we, and what are we doing?
To each and all of these questions
There is no conceivable answer.
We have suffered far more than a personal loss—
We have lost our way in the dark.

T. S. Eliot, excerpt, "The Family Reunion," from *The Complete Poems and Plays 1909–1950*, 1939

Michael Angel, *Waterfall II (Psalm 42:7)*, 2007

Psalm 22:1-8

My God, my God, why have you forsaken me?
Why are you so far from helping me,
from the words of my groaning?
O my God, I cry by day, but you do not answer;
and by night, but find no rest.

Yet you are holy,
enthroned on the praises of Israel.
In you our ancestors trusted;
they trusted, and you delivered them.

To you they cried, and were saved;
in you they trusted, and were not put to shame.

But I am a worm, and not human;
scorned by others, and despised by the people.
All who see me mock at me;
they make mouths at me, they shake their heads;
"Commit your cause to the LORD; let him deliver—
let him rescue the one in whom he delights!"

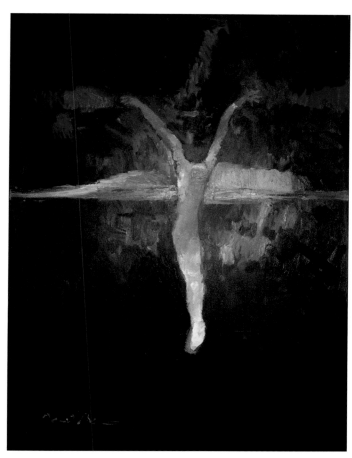

Daniel Bonnell, *Upside Down Sunset*

Meekness and majesty, manhood and Deity
in perfect harmony, the Man who is God.
Lord of eternity dwells in humanity,
kneels in humility and washes our feet.

   Oh, what a mystery—
   meekness and majesty;
   bow down and worship,
   for this is your God.

Father's pure radiance, perfect in innocence,
yet learns obedience to death on a cross,
suffering to give us life,
conquering through sacrifice,
and, as they crucify, prays, "Father, forgive."

Wisdom unsearchable, God the invisible,
Love indestructible in frailty appears.
Lord of infinity, stooping so tenderly,
lifts our humanity
to the heights of his throne.

Graham Kendrick, *Meekness and Majesty / This Is Your God*

© See Text Sources

Giotto di Bondone
(1266–1336), *Pieta
(Lamentation)*,
detail

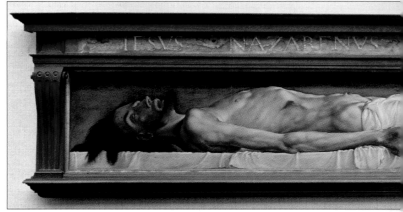

Hans Holbein the Younger,
Dead Christ, 1521

What wondrous love is this,
   O my soul! . . .
What wondrous love is this
   that caused the Lord of bliss
to bear the dreadful curse
   for my soul . . .

When I was sinking down . . .
when I was sinking down beneath
   God's righteous frown,
Christ laid aside his crown
   for my soul . . .

To God and to the Lamb,
   I will sing . . .
to God and to the Lamb,
   who is the great I AM—
while millions join the theme,
   I will sing . . .

And when from death I'm free,
   I'll sing on . . .
and when from death I'm free,
   I'll sing and joyful be,
and through eternity,
   I'll sing on . . .

Alexander Means, *What Wondrous Love Is This*, 1835

Makoto Fujimura, *Gravity and Grace*, 2002

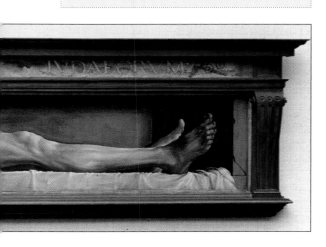

As the black door of death slides open, everlasting Light appears triumphantly!

Anneke Kaai and Eugene H. Peterson, *In a Word*, 2003

Anneke Kaai, *Death*, 2001

This is the mind-set of One who has come:
servant and helper, Savior and friend,
washing the footsore and drying the tears,
striding the highway, knowing the end—

> *Turn around, turn around*
> *all our thought, all our mind*
> *to the will of Christ, and the way of Christ,*
> *the will and the way of Christ Jesus!*

This is the mind-set of One who is born
human and hurting, blessed and cursed,
bending to burdens and lifting our loads,
healing our sickness, facing the worst—*Refrain*

This is the mind-set that goes beyond self:
grasping no glory, craving no crown,
pawn in no market, a voice for the poor,
throwing our values all upside down—*Refrain*

This is the mind-set that chose to lose face,
one with the outcast, naming God's name,
tempted and tortured, then nailed to a cross,
bleeding and crying object of shame—*Refrain*

This is the mind-set of Christ for our time:
colors and cultures loved for their worth,
stone of injustice and death rolled away,
new men and women, peace to the earth! *Refrain*

Shirley Erena Murray, *This Is the Mind-Set of One Who Has Come*

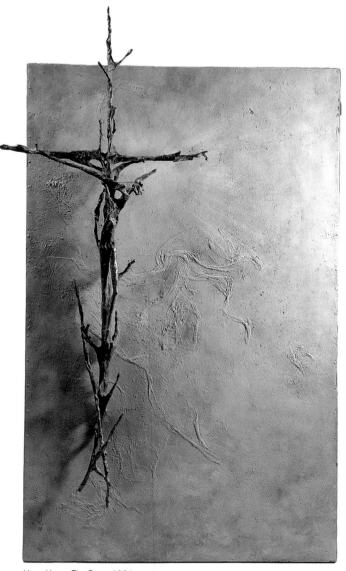

Yuyu Yang, *The Cross*, 1964

C. Robin Janning, *Some Mercy*, 2007

Baptistry window, Cathedral Church of St. Michael, Coventry, England, 1962

Down from the height of his glory he came,
willingly leaving his rightful domain:
Jesus was born in the image of man,
love was his motive and mercy his aim.

All through those days his resolve was the same—
Jesus the servant, the sharer of pain:
perfect obedience, the path of disdain,
down to a death of derision and shame.

Now God has granted him honor and fame,
taken him up to the highest to reign:
"Jesus is Lord!" every voice shall maintain,
all of creation shall bow to his name.

Michael A. Perry (1942–1996), *Down from the Height of His Glory He Came*

Folio from the Missal of Abbess de Munchensey (Christ in Glory)

Museum Mayer van den Bergh, Antwerpen © collectiebeleid.

He Qi, *The Risen Lord*, 1998

Name of all majesty, fathomless mystery,
King of the ages by angels adored;
power and authority, splendor and dignity,
bow to his mastery—Jesus is Lord!

Child of our destiny, God from eternity,
love of the Father on sinners outpoured;
see now what God has done sending his only Son,
Christ the beloved One—Jesus is Lord!

Savior of Calvary, costliest victory,
darkness defeated and Eden restored;
born as a man to die, nailed to a cross on high,
cold in the grave to lie—Jesus is Lord!

Source of all sovereignty, light, immortality,
life everlasting and heaven assured;
so with the ransomed, we praise him eternally,
Christ in his majesty—Jesus is Lord!

Timothy Dudley-Smith, *Name of All Majesty*

Laura James, *Psalm 100*, 2004

All praise to Christ, our Lord and King divine,
yielding his glory in his love's design,
that in our darkened hearts his grace might shine:
Alleluia!

Christ came to us in lowliness of thought;
by him the outcast and the poor were sought,
and by his death was our redemption bought:
Alleluia!

The mind of Christ is as our mind should be—
he was a servant, that we might be free,
humbling himself to death on Calvary:
Alleluia!

And so we see in God's great purpose how
Christ has been raised above all creatures now,
and at his name shall every nation bow:
Alleluia!

Let every tongue confess with one accord,
in heaven and earth, that Jesus Christ is Lord,
and God the Father be by all adored:
Alleluia!

F. Bland Tucker, *All Praise to Christ*, 1938

You, Lord, are both Lamb and Shepherd.
You, Lord, are both prince and slave.
You, peacemaker and swordbringer
of the way you took and gave.
You, the everlasting instant;
You, whom we both scorn and crave.

Clothed in light upon the mountain,
stripped of might upon the cross,
shining in eternal glory,
beggar'd by a soldier's toss,
You, the everlasting instant;
You, who are both gift and cost.

You, who walk each day beside us,
sit in power at God's side.
You, who preach a way that's narrow,
have a love that reaches wide.
You, the everlasting instant;
You, who are our pilgrim guide.

Worthy is our earthly Jesus!
Worthy is our cosmic Christ!
Worthy your defeat and vict'ry.
Worthy still your peace and strife.
You, the everlasting instant;
You, who are our death and life.

Sylvia G. Dunstan (1955–1993), *You, Lord, Are Both Lamb and Shepherd /
Christus Paradox*

Jan van Eyck, *The Adoration of the Lamb*, detail from the Ghent Altarpiece, 1432

God at Work

Philippians 2:12-13

Philippians 2:12-13

. . . and every tongue should confess
that Jesus Christ is Lord,
to the glory of God the Father.

[12]Therefore, my beloved, just as you have always obeyed me, not only in my presence, but much more now in my absence, work out your own salvation with fear and trembling; [13]for it is God who is at work in you, enabling you both to will and to work for his good pleasure.

Do all things without murmuring and arguing . . .

After an amazing piece of music, or at the close of a moving play, or when a speaker has truly touched the hearts of the listeners, there is often a pause—a tense silence before the applause erupts or the curtain falls, or the discussion begins. The short passage that follows Paul's hymn of praise provides a similar moment. Paul himself may have paused in the dictation of this letter, temporarily distracted by the vision of Glory, proceeding almost in a whisper. It is not too far-fetched to imagine that a holy silence fell over the gathering of Christ followers at Philippi when this great hymn had been read—a moment pregnant with promise and possibility.

Jesus said, "I am the vine, you are the branches. Those who abide in me and I in them bear much fruit, because apart from me you can do nothing."[1] Twenty-hundred years later, Dag Hammarskjöld would write, "I don't know Who—or what—put the question, I don't know when it was put. I don't even remember answering. But at some moment I did answer YES to Someone—or Something—and from that hour I was certain that existence is meaningful and that, therefore, my life, in self-surrender, had a goal."[2] God was at work.

Jesus said, "You are the salt of the earth; but if salt has lost its taste, how can its saltiness be restored?" Jesus also said, "You are the light of the world. A city built on a hill cannot be hid. No one after lighting a lamp puts it under a bushel basket. . . ."[3] Reflecting on Jesus' words in the aftermath of World War II, William Barclay would write, "Christianity is something which is meant to be seen. . . . 'there can be no such thing as secret discipleship, for either the secrecy destroys the discipleship, or the discipleship destroys the secrecy.'"[4] God was at work.

Paul wrote to the Christ followers in Ephesus, "You were dead through the trespasses and sins in which you once lived, following the course of this world. . . . But God, who is rich in mercy, out of the great love with which he loved us even when we were dead through our trespasses, made us alive together with Christ—by grace you have been saved."[5] God was at work.

Anytime a seeker becomes a Christ follower is a moment when God's love destroys secrecy. "Come and see a man who told me everything I have ever done!"[6] screamed a woman with unstoppable joy. An hour before, her personal shame forced her to travel to the community well at the "wrong" time of day to avoid her neighbors. What made the difference? God had said, through the lips of a Galilean rabbi, "I know everything there is to know about you, and I *still* love you."

Those are the words every human heart is literally dying to hear. Christ followers have been made alive with Christ—not because of anything they have done or not done, but because God in Jesus Christ is all about giving life back to dead people—industrial-strength life that will last for eternity.

When we finally realize that the "Name that is above every name" knows us by name, when we finally see in the face of God the compassionate love we have been searching for in every other face we have ever seen, it is a life-giving, life-changing, transforming discovery. We know that nothing about us will ever be the same. God is at work, in us!

This is why Paul urges us to take advantage of the moments immediately following the great hymn to dwell in the beauty of Christ, consider the promise of God in Christ, and let the reality of Christ's love and grace saturate our reality.

God is at work—in us! And we come into this moment with understandable fear and trembling. C. S. Lewis wrote, "To please God . . . to be a real ingredient in the divine happiness . . . to be loved by God, not merely pitied, but delighted in as an artist delights in his work or a father in a son—it seems impossible, a weight or burden of glory which our thoughts can hardly sustain. But so it is."[7]

Earl Palmer wrote:

> God is at work to carry out his gracious will, to make real in our lives what was the reality of Jesus' life. But we must equally be at work each day of our lives to spell out the implications. This means that we rest in the great fact that our salvation is a gift that all of our work and working could never achieve. Nevertheless we work because that salvation is so total and so complete that it demands a practical, everyday response from us. This sounds like a contradiction. But it is not.[8]

God loves "dead" people, refitting us with a life we could never have imagined. God does this because of his great love for us. This is rebirth into eternal life—God's life. A little fear and trembling is appropriate. But God is at work, calling, saving, loving, acting, inspiring, and enabling us to shine—another lamp ignited by the Light of the world.

1   John 15:5

2   Dag Hammarskjöld, *Markings*, 1964

3   Matthew 5:13a, 14-15a

4   William Barclay, *The Gospel of Matthew*, 1958

5   Ephesians 2:1-2a, 4-5

6   John 4:29a

7   C. S. Lewis, *The Weight of Glory and Other Addresses*, 1949

8   Earl F. Palmer, *Integrity*, 2000

1. *When is the last time you were truly silent, mind and heart, before God? Take several minutes for deep silence at the beginning of this reflection. How long can you focus your mind and heart on nothing but the glory of God and the grace of Jesus Christ?*

2. *How easy was it to stay focused on God alone? What distracted you?*

3. *What hold do these distractions have over you—emotional, psychological, practical? Are they the result of the demands of time or of the demands of other people, or are these distractions the result of multi-tasking and a simple lack of personal discipline?*

4. *Do distractions keep you removed from the reality of the presence of God or do they simply keep you isolated from a deeper experience of being in God's presence? What might you be missing?*

5. *What is the defining reality in your life at the moment? What is its ultimate importance? How is this "reality" defining your relationship with God?*

6. *How is God at work in your present reality to accomplish his will in your life? Where do you see the potential for expressions of agape or an experience of God's shalom?*

7. *What is God saying to you even in your most distracted moments?*

. . . work out your own salvation *with* **fear and trembling;** *for it is* **God who is at work in you . . .**

The paradoxical nature of "work out your own salvation" and "God is at work in you" has been experienced in many ordinary and extraordinary lives: Jonah, Mary Magdalene, Moses, those around the table at Emmaus, Hannah, the three Marys at the tomb . . . and in our own lives. In a sense, all of Scripture is a narrative on the nature of God's divine action in relationship to the actions of God's people.

"Work out your own salvation" here . . . is a shortened expression for "to *live* as a Christian," to *show* and *prove* oneself, what one is as a Christian. The salvation, the promised final deliverance that the Christian as such awaits, claims the movement, the activity, the work, the life of the whole [person].

Karl Barth, *The Epistle to the Philippians*, 1947

Mary Ann Osborne, *Jonah and the Whale*, 1999

Donatello, *Mary Magdalen*, 1453

Donatello's extraordinary sculpture of the *Magdalene* . . . brings before our eyes and our consciousness a vision of a once beautiful woman whose flesh has been so subdued to the spirit that little of it remains on the gaunt frame. Suffering and deprivation are written upon the face, which we at first find as hard to look upon as watching one who is dying. Yet as we enter into her being, her selflessness melts our defenses. She is wholly absorbed in another realm. Her stance shows a touching uncertainty, almost a hesitation as she steps forward. What the Magdalen lacks in physical force is more than balanced by the spiritual power of her ravaged face and tender hands. She might have been a woman of Dachau or Buchenwald. . . . The Magdalen embodies infinitely more than a courageous and noble endurance of suffering. With incredible sensitivity the artist shaped her hands to express both pleading and acceptance, the central Christian experience of faith and grace.

Jane Dillenberger, *Image and Spirit in Sacred and Secular Art*, 1990

These works, proceeding from the good root of faith, are good and acceptable to God, since they are all sanctified by his grace. Yet they do not count toward our justification—for by faith in Christ we are justified, even before we do good works. Otherwise they could not be good, any more than the fruit of a tree could be good if the tree is not good in the first place.

The Belgic Confession, 1561

Scott Sullivan, *Moses Before the Burning Bush,* 2004

The life laid down is taken up again,
the power of sin and death has lost its hold,
and we are reconciled to God through Christ:
Alleluia!

Though doubts and fears beset our hearts and minds,
the risen, wounded Savior knows our needs
and comes to meet us in the midst of life:
Alleluia!

Along life's way, the stranger and the guest
teach us anew the story of God's love;
we taste and see how Christ has fed our hearts:
Alleluia!

Sometimes we roam, not knowing we have strayed
until we find ourselves at life's raw edge
and learn that our good Shepherd guards us still:
Alleluia!

From death to life, through waters of new birth,
we are made heirs of Christ's redeeming work
and called to live as bearers of Christ's light.
Alleluia!

Carl P. Daw, Jr., *The Life Laid Down Is Taken Up Again*, 2001, rev. 2006

The tragedy of modern faith is that
we no longer are capable of being
terrified. We aren't afraid of God, we
aren't afraid of Jesus, we aren't afraid
of the Holy Spirit. As a result, we
have ended up with a need-centered
gospel that attracts thousands . . . but
transforms no one.

Michael Yaconelli (1942-2003)

Ivo Dulcic, *Meal at Emmaus*, 1971

Where the love of God is guiding
there is now another way:
New awareness of compassion
learned from one another,
    love, the face of God in Jesus,
    new creation's thrust,
    love, transforming tears and terror
    into health and trust.

Where the truth of God is driving
there is now another way,
shining through our time's confusion,
sharp with revelation:
    Words that stifle sense or spirit
    changed and redefined,
    crosses raised to teach division
    lowered, left behind.

Where the life on earth is cherished,
there is now another way,
where a child may grow in safety,
where there's peace and shelter,
    when we hold the fragile planet
    in our conscious care,
    when we see again as sacred
    all we are and share.

God will lead us on this mission,
God, the flight-path and the power,
lifting all who grasp the vision
into understanding:
    So the heart and hope within us
    set each other free,
    where the love of God is guiding,
    this shall come to be.

Shirley Erena Murray, *Where the Love of God Is Guiding*

Agnes C. Fisher, *Hannah and Her Children Dance*, 2007

With trembling bliss of eager hearts
we seek you in this place;
in private prayer and public praise
we know and sing of grace:
Complete the joy that faith can hold—
keep us in your embrace.

With awe and wonder, we still see
the nails' imprints in you;
your broken flesh and outpoured blood
bring depths of love to view:

Let heaven's bread revive our souls—
salvation's cup renew.

With fervent love you come to us,
rekindling every soul
until our hearts are strangely warmed
and broken lives are whole;
may loving you by serving all
become our joy and goal.

David A. Robb, *With Trembling Bliss of Eager Hearts*, 1990

To become aware of
the ineffable is to
part company with
words. . . . The tangent
to the curve of human
experience lies beyond
the limits of language.
The world of things we
perceive is but a veil.
Its flutter is music,
its ornament science,
but what it conceals is
inscrutable. Its silence
remains unbroken;
no words can carry it
away. . . . Sometimes
we wish our own heart
would speak of that
which made it heavy
with wonder.

Abraham Joshua Heschel, *I Asked for Wonder*, 1985

Henry Ossawa Tanner, *The Three Marys*, 1910

"Fear-of-the-Lord" is a new word in our vocabularies; it marks the way of life appropriate to our creation and salvation and blessing by God. . . . Fear-of-the-Lord is not a technique for acquiring spiritual know-how but a willed non-knowing. . . . Fear-of-the-Lord, nurtured in worship and prayer, silence and quiet, love and sacrifice, turns everything we do into a life of "breathing God."

Eugene H. Peterson, *Christ Plays in Ten Thousand Places*, 2005

Josephine Bloodgood, *Encounter*, 2002

Life Revealed

Philippians 2:14-18

Philippians 2:14-18

. . . for it is God who is at work in you, enabling you both to will and to work for his good pleasure.

14Do all things without murmuring and arguing, 15so that you may be blameless and innocent, children of God without blemish in the midst of a crooked and perverse generation, in which you shine like stars in the world. 16It is by your holding fast to the word of life that I can boast on the day of Christ that I did not run in vain or labor in vain. 17But even if I am being poured out as a libation over the sacrifice and the offering of your faith, I am glad and rejoice with all of you— 18and in the same way you also must be glad and rejoice with me.

I hope in the Lord Jesus to send Timothy to you soon, so that I may be cheered by news of you. . . .

Someone once said, if the early church had not had so many significant problems, we would not have a significant portion of the New Testament. Beyond the stories of Jesus and the story of the power of the Holy Spirit to propel the Good News into the world, the New Testament chronicles the challenges God's people have faced living a transformed life in the midst of a corrupt world, as habits and behaviors learned in the world continue in the church.

Habits, once learned, are difficult to break. When Christ followers form a community devoted to Jesus, they are still just ordinary people who have discovered a deep desire to live in a way that is pleasing to God and a witness to the truth of the Good News. Their habits and behavior can still reflect the values of a world oblivious to God. It should never be a surprise that church people are every bit as capable of hurting, deceiving, and disappointing one another as secular people.

God's people have murmured and argued their way through history. Sermons Moses preached, preserved in the book of Deuteronomy, detail the murmuring of God's people even after he freed them from slavery in a foreign land and made every provision for their safe journey home. Undistracted by God's repeated demonstrations of love and faithfulness, the people complained all the way into the land God had prepared for them. Along with stories from the days of the prophets, accounts of petty arguments among Jesus' own followers, and the problems Paul addresses in his letters, we have undeniable proof of the ability of blessed people to behave badly.

But murmuring, arguing, and complaining are just symptoms. Like all behaviors, good and bad, they point beyond themselves, revealing the attitudes of our hearts. It doesn't work to say to one another, "Quit complaining—can't you just get a life?" Audible murmuring might stop for a while, but the sin that is the root cause of the behavior will find another outlet for expression. Even when prayers and professions of faith give Christ followers words to say together like "unity" and "fellowship" and "love," sinful behaviors reveal dimensions of life that remain largely impervious to God's grace and peace. In order for these behaviors to be changed permanently, something at the level of our core convictions must be permanently changed.

How does this change happen? By the power of the Holy Spirit reminding God's children who we really are.

Murmuring originates from a perception of insignificance—a feeling of being under-valued and over-looked. In the days of Moses, God's people were freed from the brutality and humiliation of slavery, only to find themselves wandering through a wilderness, eating food that, while miraculous, was still bland and predictable, with no clear destination or purpose in sight. They felt insignificant and overlooked—forgotten by God—and they complained. Jesus' followers were arguing over which one of them would be selected for a place of honor in the kingdom Jesus kept promising. They were trying to prove to each other who was more worthy of Jesus' recognition and trust—arguing their self-significance. In both instances, God's people were behaving like immature siblings, vying for their parents' attention and love.

Actions and attitudes reveal perceptions of reality. If we believe God's affection and favor must be earned by good works and perennial niceness, it is inevitable that we will try to outdo one another in garnering God's approval. When we think we have earned it, we gloat. When we think we are being shortchanged, we fight. It is only when we begin to understand God's grace—that we already have God's unconditional love and undivided attention because of God's immense love—that we begin to experience God's peace. Murmuring and arguing stop.

When we finally begin to understand that God loves us more than we can ever possibly know, we will begin to realize we have nothing to complain about. Our deepest desires will be filled because we will desire nothing more than we desire God. And when we finally begin to realize God's unconditional love is offered with equal affection to everyone who desires it, we will be at peace with each other and with God. That is when the Good News begins to shine.

Mahatma Gandhi was a young man practicing law in South Africa when he was attracted to Jesus and considered becoming a Christ follower. One day a white elder blocked his entrance to a large church, threatening him if he did not leave. Years later, the missionary Earl Stanley Jones asked Gandhi why he rejected Christ. Gandhi replied, "Oh, I don't reject your Christ. I love your Christ. It's just that so many of you Christians are so unlike your Christ."

G. K. Chesterton once said, "The Christian ideal has not been tried and found wanting. It has been found difficult, and left untried." When Christ followers are able to overcome the worldly habits of our hearts, we shine like stars.

1. What does it mean to you that God has chosen you and calls you "dearly loved"? (Colossians 3:12, NIV) How does this truth affect the way you live your daily life?

2. Paul claims true Christ followers will shine like stars in the universe. Read John 1:1–14 carefully, then reread this passage. What does this light and darkness metaphor say to you?

3. Why does Paul make the connection between grumbling or complaining and purity before God? How does this teaching relate to "community" and "God's will"?

4. Is there a difference between the way people live in the community of your congregation and the way people live in the world outside your church? Describe the difference(s).

5. What characteristics of your congregation would be most attractive to people who have never experienced the love of Jesus Christ? What would be most off-putting?

6. How can God use you to change the ethos of your congregation?

O Lord, take our minds and think
   through them;
take our lips and speak through them;
take our lives and live out your life;
take our hearts and set them on fire
   with love for thee;
and guide us ever by thy Holy Spirit,
through Jesus Christ our Lord. Amen.

William H. M. H. Aitken (1841-1927), *The Prayer at Eventide*

Amazing God:
You create men and women in your image,
rejoicing, and proclaiming your creation good.
Your greatest desire is to love and be loved.
Thank you.

Loving God:
You call us by name, adopt us as your children,
and promise to be eternally faithful—
the only God we will ever need.
Thank you.

We do not deserve your love
because we have sinned:
We have decided to love ourselves instead of loving you,
so we plunder your world to satisfy our greed,
and exploit each other to satisfy our lust,
despising anyone who inconveniences us
and fearing anything we do not understand.

Worst of all, we are ungrateful:
We forget your love and your promise.
We murmur and gossip,
we argue and complain like spoiled children
when the world we stubbornly try to re-create in our image
reveals how shallow we truly are.

Forgiving God, have mercy on us:
You love us so completely
that your sent your Son into this rebellious world
to endure the brutality of our arrogant pride,
and be crushed to death under the weight of our sin.

By his resurrection you have reclaimed your creation.
By the power of your Holy Spirit you recover hope, restore joy,
and remind us that you are eternally faithful—
the only God we will ever need.

Please keep reminding us, until we understand:
In Jesus Christ we are forgiven. We have nothing to fear.
Glory to you, amazing God, now and forever. Amen!

Paul Detterman, 2007

*. . . children of God without blemish **in the midst of a crooked** and perverse **generation**, in which you shine like stars in the world.*

Vincent van Gogh, *The Starry Night*, 1889

Gogh, Vincent van (1853-1890). The Starry Night. 1889. Oil on canvas, 29" x 36 1/4". Acquired through the Lillie P. Bliss Bequest. (472.1941). The Museum of Modern Art, New York, NY, U.S.A. Digital Image © The Museum of Modern Art / Licensed by SCALA / Art Resource, NY.

. . . The church is the only building in the landscape that does not reflect the brilliance of the stars above. . . . Van Gogh employed the intense blue of the sky as a symbol of the divine and infinite presence. . . .

Starry Night has been analyzed at great length, perhaps more than any other of van Gogh's paintings, but few of its critics have attempted to understand the painting as a synthesis of van Gogh's ideas about religion and modernity. . . . Most fail to discuss the whole work with its three elements of village, cypress, and starry sky, and thus fail to understand its importance in describing van Gogh's whole spiritual pilgrimage, its defeat and ultimate triumph, its past and its future. . . . It is both a celebration of life and an acquiescence to impending death—with the hope that in death, he will find release and union with the infinite God.

Kathleen Powers Erickson, *At Eternity's Gate*, 1998

Alberto Giacometti, *City Square (La Place)*, 1948

Living God,
at times we are strangers on the earth,
disconcerted by the violence,
the harsh oppositions.
And you breathe upon us
the Spirit of peace like a gentle breeze.
Transfigure the deserts of our doubts
and so prepare us to be bearers of reconciliation
wherever you place us,
until a hope of peace arises in our world.

Taizé Community, *Prayer for Each Day*

Do not fear to hope
tho' the wicked rage and rise,
our God sees not as we see,
success is not the prize.
Do not fear to hope
for tho' the night be long,
the race shall not be to the swift,
the fight not to the strong.

Look to God when you are sure
your sin is greater than grace.
Look to God whose love is gift.
Believe and you can behold him face to face.
Refrain

Look to God when victory
seems out of justice' sight.
Look to God whose mighty hand
brought forth the day from the chaos of the night.
Refrain

Look to God when cynics say
our planet's doom is sealed.
Look to God by whose great pow'r
the dead were raised and the lepers were healed.
Refrain

Look to God when reason fails
and terror reigns in the night.
Look upon the Crucified
and see beyond into Easter's dawning light.
Refrain

Rory Cooney, *Do Not Fear to Hope*

Lynn Aldrich, *Island*, 1997

Beyond the beauty and the awe,
beyond the fear and dread,
we long, O God, to hear your word,
to taste your transformed bread.

Our lives feel torn between the world,
whose needs are grimly real,
and empty talk of peace and joy
with distant, vague appeal.

Oh, teach us how to hear your voice
despite the traffic's din,
to keep the blasts of rancor out
and let your Spirit in.

In sound or silence, sight or smell,
may we some token find
that makes your living presence known
to body, soul, and mind.

Then help us live as Jesus taught,
as light and salt and yeast,
that others may be brought to share
your promise and your feast.

Carl P. Daw, Jr., *Beyond the Beauty and the Awe*, 1994

Randy Beumer, *How Can I Help?* 2005

Virginio Ciminaghi, *Annunciation*, 1967

God the Sender, send us,
God the Sent, come with us,
God the Strengthener of those who go, empower us,
that we may go with you
and find those who will call you
Father, Son and Holy Spirit.

Church in Wales, from *Prayers Encircling the World*, 1998

Paul's
Humanity

Philippians 2:19-30

Philippians 2:19-30

. . . and in the same way you also must be glad and rejoice with me.

[19]I hope in the Lord Jesus to send Timothy to you soon, so that I may be cheered by news of you. [20]I have no one like him who will be genuinely concerned for your welfare. [21]All of them are seeking their own interests, not those of Jesus Christ. [22]But Timothy's worth you know, how like a son with a father he has served with me in the work of the gospel. [23]I hope therefore to send him as soon as I see how things go with me; [24]and I trust in the Lord that I will also come soon.

[25]Still, I think it necessary to send to you Epaphroditus—my brother and co-worker and fellow soldier, your messenger and minister to my need; [26]for he has been longing for all of you, and has been distressed because you heard that he was ill. [27]He was indeed so ill that he nearly died. But God had mercy on him, and not only on him but on me also, so that I would not have one sorrow after another. [28]I am the more eager to send him, therefore, in order that you may rejoice at seeing him again, and that I may be less anxious. [29]Welcome him then in the Lord with all joy, and honor such people, [30]because he came close to death for the work of Christ, risking his life to make up for those services that you could not give me.

Finally, my brothers and sisters, rejoice in the Lord. . . .

*I*t has been said, "A hero, a genius, a 'religious personality' stands alone; an apostle has others beside him like himself and sets them on his own level. He speaks in an office occupied by *many*. He can fall, but his Lord does not fall with him."[1] Paul had lived for years as a hero—a religious superstar—with a unique pedigree and infamous motives. According to the Book of Acts, he not only had personal access to the highest religious authorities in Jerusalem, but he was also well-known among the Christ followers—his reputation preceding him into many different cities and regions.[2]

Throughout these years Paul stood alone. He was a zealot—accomplished and impressive. When, by the power of God, he became an apostle, a Christ follower, it marked a radical change in his life. God accomplished this transformation by humbling him and placing this religious lone ranger within a community of equals. Paul was suddenly one of (and dependent on) the very people he had once despised and persecuted.

This was not easy to accept, for the Christ followers or for Paul. But as God said, answering the alarmed prayer of one skeptical man, ". . . [Paul] is an instrument whom I have chosen to bring my name before Gentiles and kings and before the people of Israel; I myself will show him how much he must suffer for the sake of my name."[3] Paul would indeed come to understand what it meant to suffer.

The change in Paul's life began one normal day when he was traveling from Jerusalem to Damascus. The power of the living God was revealed to him, and in that moment, he discovered it was true—the teaching he despised, perpetuated by the people he was persecuting— the Good News about Jesus the Christ, the crucified and living God, was true. It was an experience that stunned him—literally knocking him to the ground.

In the days that followed, Paul suffered. He temporarily lost his sight, suffering the indignity of helplessness and total dependence—being led around by the hand, unable to eat or drink. He suffered the ongoing humiliation of needing to rely completely on the people he had intended to destroy. And in many ways, Paul suffered alone. The Christ followers still feared him, but now the Jews also despised him, thinking he had betrayed them. No one trusted him. Paul had fallen— hard.

But God had not fallen with him. Instead, God's amazing, inverted, counterintuitive love provided Paul sanctuary among people whose shared experience of grace and peace had forged a fellowship—a community devoted to Jesus. In that community, Paul continued to experience the Good News, the undeniable power of God, and the unparalleled compassion of others. The change that began on the Damascus road became permanent. Paul's zeal for God, the energy he once had for persecuting those whose faith challenged the old standards of Jewish religious practice and allegiance, turned outward to share the Good News of Jesus Christ—alive, replicating his experience of a loving, devoted, Christ-centered community throughout the cities of the Gentile world. In Philippi, as in few other places, his teaching was eagerly applied.

Jesus had taught that anyone who wants to follow him must rearrange the priorities of life—placing the needs and concerns of others first. This had become the pattern of life in Philippi, and since it was impossible for the community of Christ followers in Philippi to care for

Paul personally, they sent Epaphroditus, a compassionate emissary, to care for Paul during his imprisonment—showing Christ's love.

We know very little about Epaphroditus. Certainly he must have had his own life and responsibilities—all of which he set aside to travel to Paul (most likely to Rome). Prisoners, even those like Paul who were under "house arrest," were not provided with much during their imprisonment. If no one brought them food and other necessities, they suffered. Apparently Epaphroditus had nearly lost his own life caring for Paul. Now, his health recovered, he was going home. His safe return would bring joy to the community that had sent him initially, and he would bring specific news (possibly even this letter) from Paul proving he was still alive and well, filled with joy and purpose.

And then there was Timothy, whom Paul introduced as one of a kind. "I have no one like him who will be genuinely concerned for your welfare. All of them are seeking their own interests, not those of Jesus Christ. But Timothy's worth you know, how like a son with a father he has served with me in the work of the gospel."[4] Timothy was not being sent to Philippi as an "heir apparent" to the ministry of Paul—an associate pastor filling in until the "superstar" was available. He was "speaking from the same office" as Paul, a true co-worker in sharing the Good News, putting the interests of Christ and Christ's people ahead of his own.

From the first word of this chapter to the last, the message is the same: true Christ followers live for others because an Other lived and died for us.

1 Karl Barth, *The Epistle to the Philippians*, 1947

2 Acts 9:1-2

3 Acts 9:15-16

4 Philippians 2:20-22

1. Which statement better characterizes your belief about working with others: "If you want something done right, do it yourself," or "The whole is greater than the sum of the parts"?

2. Are you, or do you know, someone who has had a profound experience of the power of God's transforming grace? How, specifically, has this experience changed you or them?

3. If you have never experienced a powerful example of God's transformation, what makes you believe it could happen? What makes you skeptical?

4. What do people who are not Christ followers need to see to convince them that God can change individuals and communities through the power of his love?

5. What would be an equivalent to Paul's conversion in the contemporary Church?

6. Would your congregation eagerly send someone a great distance at significant inconvenience and expense, to care for a person who was in distress? Would you allow yourself to be that person sent?

*I hope in the Lord Jesus to send Timothy to you soon, so that I may be **cheered by news of you***.

Sean Justice, *Soldier Reading Letter from Home*

Thank you to everyone for your support. It's been a little rough lately, and your letters, e-mails, and packages have all made me feel a little closer to home. 7,000 miles doesn't seem so far anymore! Anyway, continue to keep in touch and I'll try to do the same. Stay healthy, and know that I miss you all!

Sgt. Jessica Billstrom, 2004

Johannes Vermeer, *Woman Reading a Letter*, c.1662-63

Come, labor on!
Who dares stand idle, on the harvest plain
while all around us waves the golden grain?
And to each servant does the Master say,
"Go work today."

Come, labor on!
Claim the high calling angels cannot share;
to young and old the Gospel gladness bear.
Redeem the time—its hours so swiftly fly—
the night draws nigh.

Come, labor on!
The enemy is watching night and day,
to sow the tares, to snatch the seed away;
while we in sleep our duty have forgot,
he slumbers not.

Come, labor on!
Away with gloomy doubts and faithless fear!
No arm so weak but may do service here:
by feeblest agents may our God fulfill
his righteous will.

Jane L. Borthwick, *Come, Labor On*, 1859, rev. 1863

Margaret Moffett Law, *Laborers*

Welcome him *then in the Lord* **with all joy**, *and honor such people* . . .

From within this holy circle, this house of love, the mystery of God is revealed to us. It is the mystery of the three angels who appeared at the Oak of Mamre, who ate the meal Sarah and Abraham generously offered to them and who announced the unexpected birth of Isaac (Gen 18). It is the mystery of hospitality expressed not only in Abraham's and Sarah's welcome of the three angels, but also in God's welcome of the aged couple into the joy of the covenant through an heir.

Henri J. M. Nouwen, *Behold the Beauty of the Lord*, 1987

Andrei Rublev, *Icon of the Old Testament Trinity*, c.1410

Suppose you saw
the heavenly hosts
of saints and angels
praising . . . God
in the presence
of his glory . . .

You belong
to the same family
and society as they,
and are learning
their work,
and must shortly
arrive at their perfection.

Strive therefore
to imitate them
in love and joy
and let your very souls
be poured out
in praises
and thanksgiving.

Richard Baxter, *The Practical Works of the Rev. Richard Baxter*, 1830

C. Malcolm Powers,
Angelic Greeting, c. 2000-2001

Affirming Priorities

Philippians 3:1-11

Philippians 3:1-11

. . . because he came close to death for the work of Christ, risking his life to make up for those services that you could not give me.

[1]Finally, my brothers and sisters, rejoice in the Lord.

To write the same things to you is not troublesome to me, and for you it is a safeguard.

[2]Beware of the dogs, beware of the evil workers, beware of those who mutilate the flesh! [3]For it is we who are the circumcision, who worship in the Spirit of God and boast in Christ Jesus and have no confidence in the flesh— [4]even though I, too, have reason for confidence in the flesh.

If anyone else has reason to be confident in the flesh, I have more: [5]circumcised on the eighth day, a member of the people of Israel, of the tribe of Benjamin, a Hebrew born of Hebrews; as to the law, a Pharisee; [6]as to zeal, a persecutor of the church; as to righteousness under the law, blameless.

[7]Yet whatever gains I had, these I have come to regard as loss because of Christ. [8]More than that, I regard everything as loss because of the surpassing value of knowing Christ Jesus my Lord. For his sake I have suffered the loss of all things, and I regard them as rubbish, in order that I may gain Christ [9]and be found in him, not having a righteousness of my own that comes from the law, but one that comes through faith in Christ, the righteousness from God based on faith. [10]I want to know Christ and the power of his resurrection and the sharing of his sufferings by becoming like him in his death, [11]if somehow I may attain the resurrection from the dead.

Not that I have already obtained this or have already reached the goal; but I press on to make it my own, because Christ Jesus has made me his own. . . .

"Rejoice!"

At this point in the letter, Paul has made his case. God invites us into a beautiful dance: imagined by the Father, choreographed by the Son, and accompanied by the music of the Holy Spirit. This dance is just part of the inevitable outburst of joy that comes, even from the most disciplined hearts, when human beings who have been searching for honest love all our lives begin to understand that God desires an eternal relationship with us, and when we see all God is bringing to that relationship—grace and peace, promise and assurance, unconditional forgiveness, love, and unending care. God invites us to lose ourselves—to dance with uninhibited passion, and God delights when we respond! Eugene Peterson has translated Philippians 3:1, "And that's about it, friends. Be glad in God!"[1]

But, when we finally get the courage to take God's dance into our neighborhood—living as Christ followers in the reality of our daily lives—we immediately face another challenge. The music of God's joy and the heartbeat of God's love are what keep us in sync with God's eternal dance. But these can quickly be overpowered by the chaos of our world and the hammering of its demands. Seemingly relentless distractions from Grace can obliterate the music of God like the beautiful melody of a solo violin that gets lost in the roar on a subway platform each time another train passes through.

This section may begin with the word, "finally," but there is much more for Paul to teach, and more for us to learn.

Beware!

The Philippian church was young and vulnerable and, along with enthusiastic Christ followers, false teachers were there—distracting and diluting the power of the Good News. New believers eagerly received any teaching that contained even the mention of Jesus. As a result, the false teachers received a hearing along with the true disciples, and variations of Good News could spread quickly.

False teaching has taken many forms throughout the history of the Church. The false teachers in Philippi claimed that faith in Jesus Christ alone was not enough to ensure a restored relationship with God. These "dogs" were marketing gospel supplements: Christ *and* the law; Christ *and* circumcision. Faith alone, in Christ alone, was just not good enough.

Every generation has heard "Christ *and* . . ." teaching, undermining God's free gift: Christ *and* a particular method of baptism; Christ *and* membership in the correct church; Christ *and* a particular evidence of conversion; Christ *and* striving to live a "good" life. Christ followers seem inclined to want to hedge our bets just in case the truth of Christ might not be quite true enough.

Paul knew the danger of "Christ *and* . . ." teaching. If anyone held the pedigree or exhibited the enthusiasm to successfully supplement the Good News, it was Saul of Tarsus—pre-redeemed Paul. He was a man with impressive credentials in every important area of life. But when he came face to face with the living Christ, he realized his credentials meant nothing in the eyes of God. As he understood more of God's free gift of love, all his earthly efforts came to mean less than nothing to him as well.

Faith alone in Christ alone guarantees our eternal relationship with God. This was Good News for Paul. He no longer had to prove himself to God or to anyone else, but could accept God's gift of unconditional, unmerited love, and live like one who has been freed from the distraction, distortion, and disillusionment of this self-impressed world. This is Good News for us as well. But this Good News remains counterintuitive for many people, even today. How do we accept this gift? How do we listen through the hammering of "Christ *and . . .*" for the Good News—the pure music of God?

Paul had to experience Christ alive before he could believe the Good News. In the twentieth century, Karl Barth wrote, "The very boundary, the *limit* on this side of which I can understand myself only as lost, is my connection with [Christ]. . . . At this limit it is a question of knowing **the power of his resurrection**."[2]

Later in that same century, Becky Pippert wrote, "What enables us to live this new life . . . is the power unleashed by Christ's rising from the dead. He did more than die and pay the penalty of sin. He was raised from death itself, and the very power God used to raise him is the power made available to us. Through the resurrection God now offers us new life. Eternal life is the life of eternity brought forward to start in time. Living the resurrection is living in the old world by the energy of the new world to come."[3] This is the dance—the music of God transforming the chaos of our world.

How can this be? That remains the mystery—for Paul as for every other Christ follower. Paul's acknowledgement of that mystery, his vulnerability in proclaiming the reality of this Good News, allows anyone who reads this Philippian letter to stand with Paul on that outer limit—the boundary between knowledge and faith, between worldly achievement and eternal life, between absolute futility and absolute joy.

1 Eugene H. Peterson, *The Message*, 2002

2 Karl Barth, *The Epistle to the Philippians*, 1947

3 Rebecca Manley Pippert, *Hope Has Its Reasons*, 2001

1. *Why do you think a "Christ and . . ." understanding of salvation might be dangerous to growth in faith in Jesus Christ?*

2. *Paul instructs the Philippian Christ followers to "Rejoice!" saying it will safeguard them from "Christ and . . ." teaching. Why do you think this is true?*

3. *For many people, the promise of receiving God's unconditional love by faith alone is a difficult thing to believe. Why do you think that is?*

4. *What does hope mean to you? What, specifically, is the source of your greatest hope?*

5. *Where are the outer limits in your life of faith right now? What things do you know about Jesus that you do not yet trust? Do you live in hope because of your achievements or because of God's promise of eternal life?*

6. *Paul suffered the loss of everything, including all his remarkable accomplishments, for the sake of gaining Jesus Christ. Is there a significant difference between "losing" everything because of Jesus and "giving up" everything because of Jesus?*

*Finally, my brothers and sisters, **rejoice** in the Lord.*

Philippians 4:4
Rejoice in the Lord always; again I will say, Rejoice. *NRSV*

Psalm 81:2
Shout joy to God,
the God of our strength,
sing to **the God of Jacob.**

The Psalter

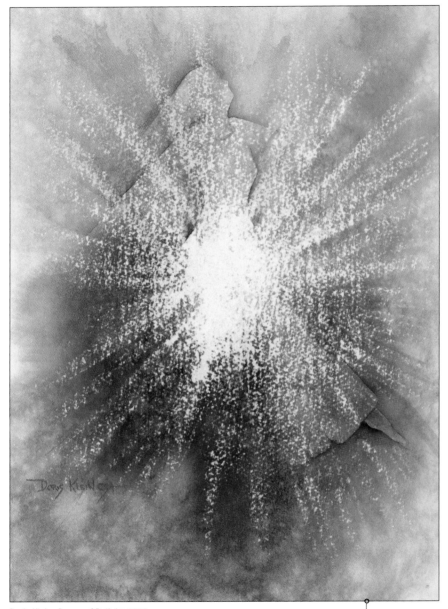

Doris Klein, *Dance of Delight*, 2000

Psalm 22:12-21

Great big bulls surround me.

And huge beasts from far away are circling in, jaws open
   like pawing, bellowing lions!

I feel like water all shook up;

my bones seem to be disintegrating;

my heart has melted like a piece of wax somewhere inside me;

my throat is terribly dry; my tongue is stuck to my mouth—

are you going to put me in the dust of death?

Because those huge dogs are all around me,

the whole dirty crowd of cutthroats are coming in for the kill:

they're going to tie me up hand and foot!

I can feel every bone—

Look! They are looking me over, looking me all over;

I know, they'll take off my clothes and throw dice
   to see who gets it—

O Lord God! Don't you go away from me . . .

Almighty One! Hurry! and help me!

Save me from the cut of death!

Spare me from those voracious dogs!

Protect me from the lion jaws!

Snatch me away from those horns of the bulls!

Calvin Seerveld, *Voicing God's Psalms*, 2005

God's people are many colors connected to the body of Christ. Here they are, dancing in a beautiful picture of partnership. Does the dancer (the bride of Christ) draw the colors in or do they flow out of the dance? "Rejoice!" means to dance as partners in Christ. It is the push and pull of partners forming their minds and their step as one. It is each member sacrificing for the other. This is real rejoicing! And what is the white light radiating from the dancer? Is it formed by all the colors joining together, or does it reflect through the dancer like a prism, showing the multicolored people of God? It is a very powerful image of the light of Christ dancing his way into our hearts.

Lord Christ, you see us
sometimes strangers on the earth,
taken aback by the violence,
by the harshness of oppositions.

And you come to send us a gentle breeze
on the dry ground of our doubts,
and so prepare us to be bearers
of peace and of reconciliation.

Brother Roger of Taizé (1915-2005), *Life from Within*

David Koloane, *Mgodoji II*, 1993

Chris Stoffel Overvoorde, *The Struggle*, 1962

Why, Lord, must evil seem to get its way?
We confess that our sin is deeply shameful;
but the wicked are openly scornful—
they mock your name and laugh at our dismay.

**We know your providential love holds true:
nothing can curse us endlessly with sorrow.
Transform, dear Lord, this damage into good;
show us your glory, hidden by this evil.**

Calvin Seerveld, excerpt, *A Congregational Lament / Why, Lord, Must Evil Seem to Get Its Way?* 1986, alt.

Lord, you said, "If you love me, you will obey what I command."
Forgive us our lukewarm love and our disobedience.

Lord, you said, "You may ask for anything in my name."
Forgive us when we think we need to solve our own problems.

Lord, you said, "Do not let your hearts be troubled and do not be afraid."
We confess that our lives are often consumed by worry and anxiety.

Lord, you said, "If you remain in me and I in you, you will bear much fruit."
Forgive us our barren lives, Lord.

Lord, you said, "You must testify, for you have been with me."
We confess, Lord, that we have been too often silent.

Lord, you said, "Love each other as I have loved you."
**In this and in so many other ways,
we confess our failures and shortcomings. Amen.**

Jessie Schut, from *Reformed Worship*, 2002

For it is we . . . who worship in the Spirit of God and boast in Christ Jesus and have **no confidence in the flesh** *. . .*

3:3-6

Karl Schmidt-Rottluff, *Pharisees*, 1912

Dear God,
silence all voices within our minds but your own.
Help us to seek and be able to follow your will.
May our prayers be joined
with those of our sisters and brothers in the faith,
that together we may glorify your name
and enjoy your fellowship forever.
In Jesus' name, Amen.

Jeffrey Carlson, from *Reformed Worship*, 1991

Fra Angelico, *St. Stephen led to torture and stoned*, 1448-49

On the right side of this fresco panel, Fra Angelico shows Saul, the onlooker (on the left), hands hidden under the cloaks of those throwing stones. This is a Saul who stands the most erect of the figures, the most sure of the action he passively participates in. (Acts 8:1)

As Paul, he writes to the people of Philippi of his experience, saying, "watch out for people who are like I once was."

In a broken and fearful world
the Spirit gives us courage
   to pray without ceasing,
    to witness among all peoples to Christ as Lord and Savior,
    to unmask idolatries in church and culture,
    to hear the voices of peoples long silenced,
    and to work with others for justice, freedom, and peace.

Excerpt, *A Brief Statement of Faith*, PC(USA)

Norman Rockwell, *The Gossips*, 1948

. . . serve God in fear and in truth, forsaking empty talkativeness and the erroneous teaching of the crowd.

Polycarp, *The Letter of Saint Polycarp, Bishop of Smyrna, to the Philippians*, early second century

Be Thou my vision, O Lord of my heart;
nought be all else to me, save that Thou art—
Thou my best thought in the day and the night,
waking or sleeping, Thy presence my light.

Riches I heed not, nor vain, empty praise,
Thou mine inheritance, now and always:
Thou and Thou only, first in my heart,
great God of heaven, my treasure Thou art.

Be Thou my wisdom, and Thou my true word;
I ever with Thee and Thou with me, Lord;
heart of my own heart, whatever befall,
still be my vision, O Ruler of all.

Unknown, *Be Thou My Vision*, 8th century

*. . . I regard everything as loss because of the **surpassing value of knowing Christ** Jesus my Lord*. . . .

3:7-9

John Wells, *Aspiring Forms*, 1950

Psalm 24:7-10
Stretch toward heaven, you gates,
open high and wide.
Let the glorious sovereign enter.

Who is this splendid ruler?
The Lord of power and might,
the conqueror of chaos.

Stretch toward heaven, you gates,
open high and wide.
Let the glorious sovereign enter.

Who is this splendid ruler?
The Lord of heaven's might,
this splendid ruler is God.

The Psalter

When we're stuck, we're much more likely to pay attention to our own hunger for God and the longings and yearnings we have stifled. Sometimes being stuck is the low point and we say, "Okay, I give up." We cannot grow without first giving up and letting go.

Michael Yaconelli, *Messy Spirituality*, 2002

My Lord, what love is this
that pays so dearly;
that I, the guilty one,
may go free?

Amazing love, O what sacrifice,
the Son of God, given for me;
my debt he pays, and my death he dies
that I might live.

And now, this love of Christ
shall flow like rivers;
come wash your guilt away.
Live again.

Graham Kendrick, *Amazing Love / My Lord, What Love Is This*
© See Text Sources

Because Jesus Christ is the Reality, the Real Factor, the Agent, in whom the lofty is humbled, the solid shattered, assurance dispelled, man in his self-made goodness exposed, Israelitic man in the splendor of his religious system declared guilty before God—because this Jesus Christ is *my Lord*, so that in effecting all this he is absolutely authoritative for me, and because he has given me to *know* that he is my Lord—*therefore* I consider the whole thing loss. . . .

Karl Barth, *The Epistle to the Philippians*, 1947

*I want to know Christ and the power of his resurrection and **the sharing** of his sufferings by becoming like him in his death . . .*

Sandra Bowden, *He Was Wounded for Our Transgressions*, 1992

Take up your cross, the Savior said,
if you would my disciple be;
deny yourself, the world forsake,
and humbly follow after me.

Take up your cross; let not its weight
fill your weak soul with vain alarm;
his strength shall bear your spirit up,
and brace your heart, and nerve your arm.

Take up your cross, nor heed the shame,
and let your foolish pride be still;
your Lord for you endured to die
upon a cross, on Calvary's hill.

Take up your cross, then, in his strength,
and calmly every danger brave:
'twill guide you to a better home
and lead to victory o'er the grave.

Take up your cross and follow Christ,
nor think till death to lay it down;
for only those who bear the cross
may hope to wear the glorious crown.

Charles William Everest, *Take Up Your Cross, the Savior Said*, 1833

Vault of the Four Seasons, Catacomb of Peter and Marcellinus, Rome, Italy, early 4th century

Even though we have four related scenes [of Jonah] . . . being dropped over the side of a boat, being swallowed by a sea monster, being spat out again, and then resting safely on land under a gourd vine . . . much has been left out of the biblical story. . . . the pictorial composition is deliberately (and consistently) selective. . . . The tradition has selected those scenes it deemed most important to bear the weight of the story's meaning and significance. . . . these images don't appear on the walls of a church or the classroom for catechumens; they appear on the walls of a tomb, near the Good Shepherd. . . . Since, according to Christian teaching and practice, death and resurrection into Paradise are achieved through the waters of baptism, the imagery can be interpreted as a reference to that rite of initiation. . . . The iconography sends a message: the soul of the dead is blissfully resting in heaven because the promise of baptism has been realized.

Robin M. Jensen, *The Substance of Things Seen*, 2004

Derek Wadlington, *Baptismal Reflections*, Campbell Hall Chapel of Columbia Theological Seminary, Decatur, Georgia, 2005

Romans 6:3–5

That's what baptism into the life of Jesus means. When we are lowered into the water, it is like the burial of Jesus; when we are raised up out of the water, it is like the resurrection of Jesus. Each of us is raised into a light-filled world by our Father so that we can see where we're going in our new grace-sovereign country.

Eugene H. Peterson, *The Message*, 2002

Perpetual God, unchanging source
of all we have and are to be:
to give yourself you were remade
a man, from death to set us free.
Now let us offer up to you
our lives, our selves as worship true.

Unleavened God, fermenting worlds
from birth to death in time and space:
convert our lives, remold our minds,
uplift us from the commonplace.
As Adam was built up from clay,
redeem us from our worldly ways.

Clandestine God, unnamed "I AM,"
revealed in Christ on Hebron's hill:
direct our metamorphosis,
transfigure us to know your will.
Unveil the treasures in our hearts.
Divulge, within our lives, your art.

Fantastic God, debased and bowed,
incarnate sacrifice Divine:
subdue our soaring selfishness
that we might serve your grand design.
All in our faith, each with a role,
shall be Christ's body strong and whole.

Impetuous heirs of steadfast grace,
grow unto love and hope and joy,
pray blessings on our enemies,
our gifts toward others' needs employ.
Let us, like choirs of seraphim,
become our God's eternal hymn.

James Hart Brumm, *Perpetual God, Unchanging Source*, 1988

© 2010 Wayne Leupold Editions, Inc.

All I once held dear, built my life upon,
all this world reveres, and wars to own;
all I once thought gain I have counted loss,
spent and worthless now, compared to this.

Knowing you, Jesus, knowing you,
there is no greater thing.
You're my all, you're the best,
you're my joy, my righteousness;
and I love you, Lord.

Now my heart's desire is to know you more,
to be found in you and known as yours,
to possess by faith what I could not earn:
all-surpassing gift of righteousness.

Oh, to know the pow'r of your risen life,
and to know you in your sufferings;
to become like you in your death, my Lord,
so with you to live and never die.

Graham Kendrick, *Knowing You / All I Once Held Dear*
© See Text Sources

Burning Mystery is set within the context of the worship space—near the table of the Lord's Supper. The movement from death to life, made possible through our unity in Christ and celebrated at the Lord's Supper, is reflected in the actual rising movement of the lower section of red and yellow silk (held up by fish line that is pulled from behind). The red color reminds us of Christ's sacrifice while also taking on a flame-like form to represent the role the Holy Spirit plays in our unity in Christ. The white section, highlighted by the blue background, reaches up vertically, echoing this movement even when the piece hangs freely.

Alice Brinkman, *Burning Mystery*, 2003

162

Philippians 3:7-11
But even more than that,
   I consider everything to be a lost cause compared to the superlative excellence of
   knowing Christ Jesus my Lord,
         through whom I lost everything I had,
               even concluding it was dung,
                     so that instead I could gain Christ and be found in him,
                     not having my own righteousness through law
                     but through faith in Christ and so getting a
                     righteousness from God through faith,
                           knowing him and the power of his
                           resurrection and the fellowship of his
                           suffering, taking on his form of death, and even,
                           somehow,
                                 arriving at the goal of the
                                 resurrection from the dead.

Scott E. Hoezee, "The Movement of Philippians 3," 2005

Elizabeth Steele Halstead, *The Tomb*, 2002

I believe in . . . the resurrection of the body.

Apostles' Creed, c. A.D. 700

The deep darkness of this painting reflects the total sacrifice of Jesus Christ. The hints of bright red paint coming down from the top (and hidden within the rock) represent Christ's shed blood.

The power of using deep blue tones has been spoken of by Wassily Kandinsky: "first in its physical movements (1) of retreat from the spectator, (2) of turning in upon its own center. The inclination of blue to depth is so strong that its inner appeal is stronger when its shade is deeper. Blue is the typical heavenly color. The ultimate feeling it creates is one of rest. When it sinks almost to black, it echoes a grief that is hardly human." (Wassily Kandinsky, *Concerning the Spiritual in Art*, 1977)

At the same moment you view the darkness of the piece you are also captured by the hope seen in the light as it breaks forth from the interior of the tomb, cracking the rock wide open. The renewed relationship between heaven and earth, depicted in the movement of vertical and horizontal lines, is made possible through Christ's resurrection. The tomb becomes a place in which we are reminded that death meets life and, with the mourning women, we realize Jesus Christ is not here yet present with us. Living, and dancing in, this moment of mystery is what Paul attains and hopes for those in Philippi and all followers of Christ.

Rise heart; thy Lord is risen. Sing his praise
                            Without delays,
Who takes thee by the hand, that thou likewise
                            With him mayst rise:
That, as his death calcined thee to dust,
His life may make thee gold, and much more, just.

Awake, my lute, and struggle for thy part
                            With all thy art.
The crosse taught all wood to resound his name,
                            Who bore the same.
His stretched sinews taught all strings, what key
Is best to celebrate this most high day.

Consort both heart and lute, and twist a song
                            Pleasant and long:
Or, since all musick is but three parts vied
                            And multiplied,
O let thy blessed Spirit bear a part,
And make up our defects with his sweet art.

George Herbert, "Easter," 1633, from *The Works of George Herbert*

In the winter of our spirits,
cold winds chill the very soul.
Trees bereft of fruit and color
cannot hearten or console.

In the winter of our spirits,
snow squalls come, obscure our sight;
yet there in the dim white distance
shines a cold, but hopeful light.

And in the winter of our spirits,
grace and faith come to suffice
with the confidence of water
flowing on beneath the ice.

To the winter of our spirits
God comes: chill winds have no sting,
and our souls, warmed by God's presence,
wait the coming of the spring.

John Core, *In the Winter of Our Spirits*, 2005

Makoto Fujimura, *The White Tree*, 2000

Unpacking the Mystery

Philippians 3:12-14

Philippians 3:12-14

. . . if somehow I may attain the resurrection from the dead.

[12]Not that I have already obtained this or have already reached the goal; but I press on to make it my own, because Christ Jesus has made me his own. [13]Beloved, I do not consider that I have made it my own; but this one thing I do: forgetting what lies behind and straining forward to what lies ahead, [14]I press on toward the goal for the prize of the heavenly call of God in Christ Jesus. Let those of us then who are mature be of the same mind; and if you think differently about anything, this too God will reveal to you. . . .

The resurrection of Jesus Christ is the central belief of the Christian faith, the triumph of God over worldly powers; the victory of Christ over death—a death he had to die to pay the price of human disobedience; the joy of Christ in a sacrifice made so we could once again delight in God. We will never fully comprehend the enormity of our need for Christ's death and resurrection, and while we remain in our earthly life, we will only catch a momentary glimpse of the joy of a restored relationship with God. But the Resurrection is the boundary between knowledge and faith, between worldly achievement and eternal life, between absolute futility and absolute joy. It is both ultimate truth and profound mystery.

Human beings are relational. Our self-image and our sense of self-worth are largely defined by the love and approval we receive from others. Children learn at a very young age what pleases and holds the attention of their parents. In school, the influence of teachers and peers becomes evident. As relationships deepen, so does our need for acceptance, affirmation, and love. Those whose opinions we care most about "take hold" of us for a season. Their values and priorities shape us. Their happiness and approval become our goal.

Jesus taught wise people to build their life on solid ground, not on shifting sand. When we look to other human beings for love and approval, the ground on which we build our life will be constantly shifting. Only when we look beyond human relationships to One who is "the same yesterday and today and forever"[1] will we find a solid foundation of unconditional love and approval.

The only unchanging One in creation is the Creator who has been revealed to us in Jesus Christ. Following Christ means allowing Christ to "take hold" of us—to be the only one whose love and approval really matter. This is not a casual decision. As Scott Hoezee comments, "When Christ takes hold of you, it is an experience so rich that it will take you the rest of eternity to figure out what you have received."

Christ had "taken hold" of Paul. Even as he wrote this letter, Paul knew he had not begun to unpack the mystery of all that that meant. Yet, the closer Paul came to Christ, the more he wanted to be with Christ. With echoes of the Resurrection drowning out the powerful voices of his past, Paul was living into a future that would only become more breathtaking the closer he came to its Redeemer.

Paul's relationship with Christ was not perfect. As he would later write, "I do not understand my own actions. For I do not do what I want, but I do the very thing I hate. . . . Now if I do what I do not want, it is no longer I that do it, but sin that dwells within me. . . . Who will rescue me from this body of death? Thanks be to God through Jesus Christ our Lord!"[2] Partnership with Christ was Paul's goal. The mystery of Christ's resurrection made that goal attainable. Discerning the Holy Spirit's leading in achieving that partnership defined Paul's spiritual journey. And this was not Paul's choice, any more than it is the choice of any human being to love God first.

Many people want a spiritual journey that more closely resembles a trip to the corner store than an epic adventure. Christian faith sounds simple. We affirm it. The teachings of Jesus sound helpful. We make a note to try them. The call to discipleship, becoming faithful Christ followers, sounds challenging but worthwhile.

Perhaps we try it, at least until other challenges distract us or the next "worthwhile" adventure comes along.

When Christ "takes hold" of us, however, everything changes. Jesus Christ, resurrected and alive, becomes the Object of our affection, the Source of our identity, and the only One whose love and approval matter. This is partnership with Christ—the epic begins.

At one level, partnership with Christ means an experience of Grace. "This is the kind of love we are talking about—not that we once upon a time loved God, but that he loved us and sent his Son as a sacrifice to clear away our sins and the damage they've done to our relationship with God."[3] In any human relationship, and in every other religion, we work to earn the attention and approval of the object of our affection. Only in partnership with Christ do we discover that the Object of ultimate affection has patiently worked to win us.

At another level, partnership with Christ assures the gift of peace. Human relationships will always be imbalanced. We are stronger, smarter, and more accomplished than some people, and we feel superior to them. Other people are stronger, brighter, and more successful than we will ever be. We envy them. Only when it is Christ whose affection and approval are all that matter is our honor so great that we can never again question our self-worth, and the price he paid for our love so great that we can never again feel superior to anyone.

1 Hebrews 13:8b

2 Romans 7:15, 20, 24b-25

3 1 John 4:10 (Eugene H. Peterson, *The Message*, 2002)

1. *What difference does it make in your daily life that Jesus Christ was raised from death?*

2. *What does it mean to you that God in Jesus Christ "takes hold" of you? Is it encouraging to know that God does not expect us to reach the goal of a completed life in Christ?*

3. *In what ways do you think such a steady, realistic, and ongoing journey of faith could be misunderstood?*

4. *What, from your past life or in your present reality, keeps you from eagerly participating in the epic adventure of faith in Jesus Christ?*

5. *What is the difference between running away from your past and running toward your new future in Jesus Christ?*

6. *How has Jesus Christ "taken hold" of you personally? What is there about Jesus that you would more fully like to explore, to understand, or to trust?*

. . . I press on *to make it my own, because Christ Jesus has made me his own.*

Eternal God,
you call us to ventures
of which we cannot see the ending,
by paths as yet untrodden,
through perils unknown.
Give us faith to go out with courage,
not knowing where we go,
but only that your hand is leading us
and your love supporting us;
through Jesus Christ our Lord.
Amen.

Eric Milner-White and George Wallace Briggs, *Daily Prayer*, 1941

Guide my feet while I run this race
Guide my feet while I run this race
Guide my feet while I run this race
for I don't want to run this race in vain!

Hold my hand . . .
Stand by me . . .
I'm your child . . .
Search my heart . . .
Guide my feet . . .

Unknown, *Guide My Feet* (African American spiritual)

Psalm 121:1
I look up to the mountains;
    does my strength come from the mountains?
No, my strength comes from GOD,
    who made heaven, and earth, and mountains.

Eugene H. Peterson, *The Message*, 2002

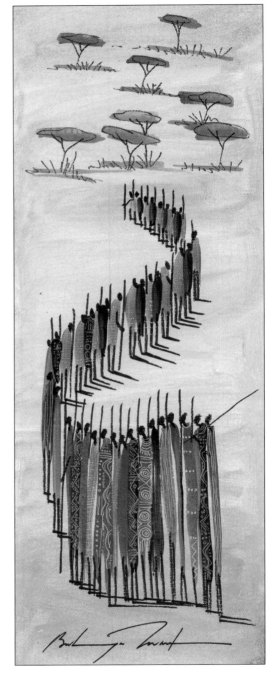

Martin Bulinya,
On the March 2

Carved of Carrara marble, this bas relief diptych represents the Women of the Resurrection: Mary the friend, Mary Magdalene announcing the news of the Resurrection, and Mary the Mother receiving and proclaiming the News.

M. J. Anderson, sculptor, 2005

M. J. Anderson, *Witness: Women of the Resurrection*, Church of the Resurrection, Solon, Ohio, 2005

Michelangelo Merisi da Caravaggio,
Incredulity of Saint Thomas, 1601-02

Psalm 130:5-6
For the Lord my soul awaits;
   In God's word, my hope is laid;
As the sentries by the dawn
   For their patience are repaid.

Michael Morgan, *The Psalter for Christian Worship*, 1999

Forgetting what lies behind and pressing on to the future,
come what may, we are resolved to reach every corner of our nation
with the Gospel of our Lord Jesus Christ.

You who are full of strength,
call your people and put in their hearts zeal for evangelism.
Enable us as a church to train and equip those you have called.
Clothe them with your Spirit,
empower us to proclaim Jesus King of all kings.

The blood of the martyrs cannot allow us to rest
when many of our brothers and sisters know no salvation.

O God, you are our hiding place.
Go before us and soften the hearts of all these thy children
whom the evil one has enslaved.

We put all our yearnings and cries before you
with full assurance that you will not throw us out.
But that you rejoice greatly when we fall on our knees
and present our requests which you are ever ready to grant,
through Jesus Christ our Lord and Redeemer.

Church in Uganda, from *Prayers Encircling the World*, 1998

Communion of Saints, Cathedral of Our Lady of the Angels, Los Angeles, California, 2001-2002

Ahead of us, a race to run:
so, looking at the past no more,
forgetting what has gone before,
we fix our eyes on God the Son—
with eager diligence to train
as for the prize ahead we strain,
until at last our course is done.

He calls us now to run the race,
discarding every weight and load
to speed our way along the road;
the path we tread, the way of grace—
and though the journey may be long,
the grace of God will keep us strong
until we stand before his face.

Martin E. Leckebusch, *Ahead of Us, A Race to Run*

God of Light,
We have been so blind when truth has been so clear.
When we could have looked ahead we fell behind.
When we could have viewed the wider picture we saw only a part.
When we could have sensed the Spirit leading we missed the way.

Forgive our dim apprehension of love's clear leading.
Give us faith that trusts when it cannot see,
through the Light that lingers when all else fails,
even the Bright and Morning Star of our faith,
Jesus Christ, the Savior.
Amen.

E. Lee Phillips, *Breaking Silence Before the Lord*, 1986

O God, our help in ages past,
our hope for years to come,
our shelter from the stormy blast,
and our eternal home:

Under the shadow of Thy throne
Thy saints have dwelt secure;
sufficient is Thine arm alone,
and our defense is sure.

Before the hills in order stood
or earth received its frame,
from everlasting Thou art God,
to endless years the same.

A thousand ages in Thy sight
are like an evening gone,
short as the watch that ends the night
before the rising sun.

O God, our help in ages past,
our hope for years to come,
still be our guard while troubles last,
and our eternal home.

Isaac Watts, *O God, Our Help in Ages Past*, 1719

Eager Hope

Philippians 3:15–21

Philippians 3:15-21

15Let those of us then who are mature be of the same mind; and if you think differently about anything, this too God will reveal to you. 16Only let us hold fast to what we have attained.

17Brothers and sisters, join in imitating me, and observe those who live according to the example you have in us. 18For many live as enemies of the cross of Christ; I have often told you of them, and now I tell you even with tears. 19Their end is destruction; their god is the belly; and their glory is in their shame; their minds are set on earthly things. 20But our citizenship is in heaven, and it is from there that we are expecting a Savior, the Lord Jesus Christ. 21He will transform the body of our humiliation that it may be conformed to the body of his glory, by the power that also enables him to make all things subject to himself.

At this point, a thoughtful person encountering Paul's teaching might ask, "What is the 'goal' of partnership with Christ? What is Paul so eager to 'make his own'?" Christ followers, at various points on their spiritual journey, will answer differently. Cornelius Plantinga has written:

> Some people expect very little from salvation, and they get it. They expect God's salvation to cure a few of their bad habits and to help them live more decently. They expect to be able to believe the right doctrines without raising any question about them. And they expect God to be night watchman over their possessions until they die and go to heaven.
>
> Others seem to expect too much—or, at any rate, too much too early. These are people who expect sinlessness or the wealth of heaven or rest from their labors or unceasing ecstasy. They want glory now.[1]

Selah.

Paul stresses the importance of unity among Christ followers; unity in mind and in heart. But unity requires commitment to a common goal—a shared worldview that is far more objective and didactic than simple agreement within a system of beliefs. This would not seem to be good news to people living in a world infused with pluralism, and yet, from the time of the New Testament on, the Good News flourishes in the most pluralistic cultures.

Expectation of unified devotion demands an exceptional reward—a prize of such intrinsic value that, when autonomous human beings finally apprehend it, they gladly sacrifice any illusion of personal independence in order to attain it. The extraordinary reward of the Good News is hope.

What is this hope that can unite disparate people into a fellowship? Becky Pippert answers:

> People have two things in common: We all want to be happy and we all want to be loved. . . . the resurrection tells us that we are spiritual beings whose true nature is discovered and fulfilled only as we live in intimacy with God. . . . [Christians] know that . . . [God] is never thwarted or caught napping by the circumstances of our lives. To have faith in Jesus does not mean we try to pretend that bad things are really good. Rather, we know that God will take our difficulties and weave them into purposes we cannot see as yet. And when he is done, the day will be more glorious for our having gone through the difficulties.[2]

Selah.

What does it mean to be saved? Stuart Briscoe has written, ". . . anyone reading anything written by Paul will understand the immensity of his understanding of 'salvation.' It was a doctrine of emancipation from anything and everything that keeps a man or woman from being what God intended them to be." That is what we have already attained—freedom, literally emancipation, from slavery to *anything and everything* that keeps us from God. This freedom is the essential gift of Jesus Christ.

Selah.

Briscoe continues, "Christians have a unique role to play. They are intended to be 'earth people,' which they are by birth, and 'heaven people,' which they are by new birth, both at the same time. This means that they are people of two realms living in one of those realms. Their role is to tell the realm where they live what the other realm is like. . . . they live on earth to bring a touch of heaven wherever they go."[3]

Selah.

Bringing a "touch of heaven" can seem a beautiful challenge or not, depending on our openness to a non-cynical consideration of God's mission and our role in it. What separates the ideal vision of Christian witness from the street-level experience of ministry for most of us? The allure and the immediacy of "earthy" life in the earthly realm, and the cunning and tenacity of the Enemy of Christ whose power deceives and distracts, keeping us content with a perpetual state of spiritual adolescence—enticing us to live for immediate satisfaction, emotional satiation, and sensual fulfillment. As "people of the two realms," Christ followers must prize unity in Christ—literally sharing the mind of Christ, to fulfill our mission of remembering what the "other realm" is like.

Selah.

Every Christ follower has "already attained" dual citizenship, knowing there is more to life than meets our immediate gaze. P. T. Forsyth once said, "If within us, we find nothing over us, we will succumb to what is around us."[4] But when the Good News has emancipated us from the lie that this world is all there is, when hope has been freed from the tyranny of the earthly realm, when, as Craig Barnes has said, ". . . [we] enjoy a world where grace is a frequent invader,"[5] we begin to realize, or is it remember, that our true citizenship is in heaven, and we wait with eager hope to see what God will do next.

Selah.

1 Cornelius Plantinga, Jr., *Beyond Doubt*, 2002

2 Rebecca Manley Pippert, *Hope Has Its Reasons*, 2001

3 Stuart Briscoe, *Philippians*, 1993

4 P. T. Forsyth, in M. Craig Barnes, *An Extravagant Mercy*, 2003

5 M. Craig Barnes, *An Extravagant Mercy*, 2003

1. *What is the goal of "partnership with Christ" for you? Based on Plantinga's quote, are you expecting too much or too little from your faith?*

2. *How would you briefly define the "worldview" of Christ followers? What common Christian beliefs unite people of different cultures, conditions, and races in a single hope?*

3. *What do you think about when you have nothing you must think about? To what does your mind "default"? What do you do with your Selah moments?*

4. *Would you describe yourself as a hope-filled person? What gives you hope?*

5. *If, as Becky Pippert suggests, human beings all want to be happy and want to be loved, how does belief in a resurrected but still intangible Savior fulfill those desires?*

6. *If, for some reason, Christ followers were to reject the biblical truth of the Resurrection, what difference would it make in the Christian witness to a pluralistic world?*

. . . observe those who live according to the example you have in us. For **many live as enemies of the cross** *. . .*

Psalm 14:1
Fools say in their hearts, "There is no
    God."
They are corrupt, they do
    abominable deeds;
there is no one who does good. *NRSV*

Psalm 54:1-4
God, for your sake, help me!
   Use your influence to clear me.
Listen, God—I'm desperate.
   Don't be too busy to hear me.

Outlaws are out to get me,
   hit men are trying to kill me.
Nothing will stop them;
   God means nothing to them.

Oh, look! God's right here helping!
   God's on my side. . . .

Eugene H. Peterson, *The Message*, 2002

Patricia Nix, *Fool*, 2001

182

Hieronymus Bosch, *The Prodigal Son*, 1500-1502

When we walk alone and work for self,
when we make our plans just to increase our wealth,
needy neighbors there by the roadside cry,
but we pass them by and take the other side.

> *Free us to serve, yes free us to serve;*
> *all in Christ are free to serve.*

But the lonely road leads to slavery—
life is full of fear, the end we cannot see;
Christ has set us free, he has shown us the way—
loving, serving others brings us liberty. *Refrain*

Every passer-by is a friend to love,
every one in need, someone in Christ to serve;
fair society, human unity—
love is means and end, and loving sets us free! *Refrain*

Tom Colvin, *Free to Serve / When We Walk Alone and Work for Self*

Here I am, the one who turned away from my God:
how stubborn my resistance!
What shall I do to find forgiveness now?
Now I pray and seek the loving kindness of God.

Darkness swallowed hope as I continued to sin:
how frightening the darkness!
Far from my home, I was bewildered, lost.
Now I go forth in the light God gave back to me.

All around, the landscape shines with new light and life,
the fields and mountains glisten!
Jesus' salvation fills the world with joy.
I will praise and sing God's goodness while I have breath.

Yukiko Ishiyama, Japan; tr. Yasuhiko Yokosaka, *Here I Am / Kata ku nani mo*

Edvard Munch, *The Scream*, 1893

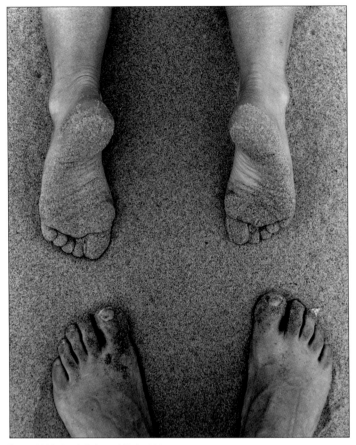

Roger M. Varland, *Cain and Abel*, 1996

Far from home we run, rebellious,
seeking cities bright with dreams,
casting loose from love that claims us,
craving life that glitters, gleams.

Dreams that lured us on have vanished;
freedom's road has run its course.
All that glittered now lies tarnished,
robbed of joy by guilt, remorse.

Long the road that winds us homeward,
faint the hope that love still waits;
yet the feet that once were wayward
lead us toward familiar gates.

Swift, a father runs to meet us,
bearing love that covers shame.
Sin and guilt no more defeat us;
grace restores a home, a name.

Arms, long empty, close around us,
binding hearts in warm embrace.
Love we'd lost once more has found us,
shines again from face to face.

Bread and wine for celebration
on the table now are spread.
Songs ascend in jubilation,
for we live who once were dead!

Herman G. Stuempfle, Jr., *Far from Home We Run Rebellious*, 1993

Psalm 84

How lovely is your dwelling place,
  O Lord of hosts!
My soul longs, yes, faints
  for the courts of the Lord;
my heart and flesh sing for joy
  to the living God.

Even the sparrow finds a home,
  and the swallow a nest for herself,
  where she may lay her young,
at your altars, O Lord of hosts,
  my King and my God.
Blessed are those who dwell in your house,
  ever singing your praise! *Selah*

Blessed are those whose strength is in you,
  in whose heart are the highways to Zion.
As they go through the Valley of Baca
  they make it a place of springs;
  the early rain also covers it with pools.
They go from strength to strength;
  each one appears before God in Zion.

O Lord God of hosts, hear my prayer;
  give ear, O God of Jacob! *Selah*

Behold our shield, O God;
  look on the face of your anointed!

For a day in your courts is better
  than a thousand elsewhere.
I would rather be a doorkeeper in the house of my God
  than dwell in the tents of wickedness.
For the Lord God is a sun and shield;
  the Lord bestows favor and honor.
No good thing does he withhold
  from those who walk uprightly.
O Lord of hosts,
  blessed is the one who trusts in you! *ESV*

Anneke Kaai, *Psalm 84*, 1996

My life flows on in endless song;
above earth's lamentation
I hear the sweet though far-off hymn
that hails a new creation:

> No storm can shake my inmost calm,
> while to that Rock I'm clinging.
> Since Christ is Lord of heaven and earth,
> how can I keep from singing?

Through all the tumult and the strife
I hear the music ringing;
it finds an echo in my soul—
How can I keep from singing?

What though the tempest 'round me roar?
I hear the truth it liveth;
what though the darkness 'round me close,
songs in the night he giveth:

The peace of Christ makes fresh my heart,
a fountain ever springing:
all things are mine since I am his—
How can I keep from singing?

Robert Lowry, *My Life Flows On in Endless Song / How Can I Keep from Singing?*, 1869

William Grosvenor Congdon, *Ego sum*, 1961

186

Jesus, still lead on, till our rest be won;
and, although the way be cheerless,
we will follow, calm and fearless;
guide us by your hand to the promised land.

If the way be drear, if the foe be near,
let no faithless fears o'ertake us,
let not faith and hope forsake us;
safely past the foe to our home we go.

When we seek relief from a long-felt grief,
when temptations come alluring
make us patient and enduring;
show us that bright shore where we weep no more.

Jesus, still lead on, till our rest be won;
heav'nly Leader, still direct us,
still support, console, protect us,
till we safely stand in the promised land.

Nicolaus L. von Zinzendorf, *Jesus, Still Lead On*, 1721

Ephesians 1:17, 2:19-22
I pray that the God of our Lord Jesus Christ, the Father of glory, may give you a spirit of wisdom and revelation as you come to know him.

So then you are no longer strangers and aliens, but you are citizens with the saints and also members of the household of God, built upon the foundation of the apostles and prophets, with Christ Jesus himself as the cornerstone. In him the whole structure is joined together and grows into a holy temple in the Lord; in whom you also are built together spiritually into a dwelling place for God.

. . . if we are pleasing [to God] in the present age, we shall also obtain the age to come, inasmuch as he promised to raise us from the dead. And if we bear our citizenship worthy of him, "we shall also reign with him"—provided, of course, that we have faith.

Polycarp, *The Letter of Saint Polycarp, Bishop of Smyrna, to the Philippians*, early second century

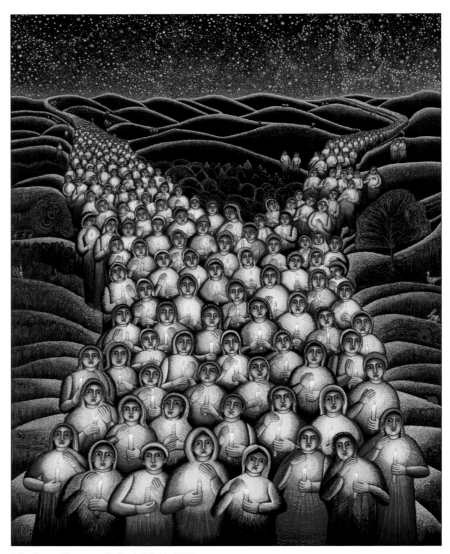

John August Swanson, *Festival of Lights*, 2000

In the Lord

Philippians 4:1–7

Philippians 4:1-7

. . . He will transform the body of our humiliation that it may be conformed to the body of his glory, by the power that also enables him to make all things subject to himself. ¹Therefore, my brothers and sisters, whom I love and long for, my joy and crown, stand firm in the Lord in this way, my beloved.

²I urge Euodia and I urge Syntyche to be of the same mind in the Lord. ³Yes, and I ask you also, my loyal companion, help these women, for they have struggled beside me in the work of the gospel, together with Clement and the rest of my co-workers, whose names are in the book of life.

⁴Rejoice in the Lord always; again I will say, Rejoice. ⁵Let your gentleness be known to everyone. The Lord is near. ⁶Do not worry about anything, but in everything by prayer and supplication with thanksgiving let your requests be made known to God. ⁷And the peace of God, which surpasses all understanding, will guard your hearts and your minds in Christ Jesus.

Finally, beloved, whatever is true, whatever is honorable, whatever is just, whatever is pure, whatever is pleasing, whatever is commendable, if there is any excellence and if there is anything worthy of praise, think about these things. . . .

Christ followers at the start of the twenty-first century have learned how much the world watches God's people behave under stress. These have been turbulent times. Hundreds of clergy sex scandals have shaken the Roman Catholic Church. Many high-profile evangelical leaders have struggled with moral failure. Mainline denominations are battling over issues of biblical fidelity. Local congregations argue over styles of worship and music. Dissent and disagreements are everywhere.

This is the Church—the Body of Christ, the representation of Jesus Christ until his promised return, the incarnation of God's love and grace. Christ's followers must always be careful and intentionally biblical about dealing with stress and disagreement, like the battle that was going on between two Philippian women.

Euodia and Syntyche, baptized fellowship members, were arguing, and their argument affected the whole Philippian community. While their disagreement was significant enough to warrant Paul's attention, the details will never be known beyond the bounds of the Philippian fellowship. No one needs to know what started this problem. Christ followers throughout ensuing generations have needed to know how it needed to be resolved.

Enter Paul the pastoral counselor. He didn't take sides or play favorites. It was not important who won but that the community remain one in Christ. And so Paul outlined a path toward reconciliation as applicable today as it was on first hearing in Philippi.

Paul's outline followed the exact pattern of his letter. God had begun a good work in these women—they were coworkers with Paul in sharing the Good News. They had experienced encouragement and comfort, fellowship and tenderness within the community of Christ followers.

They had experienced God's love. Because of their common experience of grace and peace, their dispute could be seen for what it really was—and settled before it divided the whole community.

The call and commission of Jesus Christ is not to *go to church* or even to *be part of a church*—it is to *be* church—to *be* the Body of Christ in times of agreement and in times of stress, when the Good News is flourishing and when it seems to be struggling, when Christ followers can rejoice and when God's people must be the first to confess wrong behaviors. This is the charge Paul gives to the women—and to the devoted fellowship who surrounded them.

The community has a crucial role to play. When Christ followers argue, their disputes cannot remain a personal matter. Moisés Silva wrote, "These courageous women . . . needed the assistance of the whole church to resolve their differences; brothers and sisters must not avoid intervening in the dispute simply because they are afraid of 'meddling.' Though Paul in this letter does not use the figure of the body [of Christ] with reference to the church . . . one would be hard-pressed to find a more striking illustration of that principle than the request of Philippians 4:3."[1]

Unity in mind and in purpose is a gift from the Holy Spirit. In *The Cost of Discipleship* Dietrich Bonhoeffer wrote, "[Christ] stands between us and God, and for that very reason he stands between us and all other [people] and things."[2] Going further, Earl Palmer wrote,

> . . . Because of Jesus Christ we as Christians are not left alone to figure out and to solve our interpersonal relationships as if our direct relationships with other fallible and imperfect human beings were all we have. . . . because of Christ the Savior Lord and his radical

intervention, we now have *mediated* relationships with each other in the family of faith as well as *mediated* relationships toward those outside faith and indeed toward the whole created order.[3]

It is no accident of dictation that the very next instruction from Paul resumes an earlier, though interrupted thought . . . "Rejoice—be glad in God!" Christ's followers are able to live in community defined by gentleness and by unity precisely because the Lord is near. And this gentleness must be visible to everyone—inside and outside the Church.

Experiencing the same love from God, being one in spirit and in purpose, serving others without concern for personal cost, this is what defines Christ followers—being focused on fulfilling God's desires rather than being concerned about satisfying personal desires. This change of focus is simple but it is not easy. No matter how difficult it may seem, for the sake of the Good News, it is essential.

Sarah Cunningham, a young Christ follower, has written:

Through his teaching and example, Jesus shaped his friends into a community that merged the spiritual world with reality. In contrast to the temple, it was in the presence of Jesus and his followers that people would come into contact with God. . . . If Jesus told us from day one that the church was going to prevail—and if the church has already survived more than two thousand years of flaws since Peter began preaching his first sermons—I think it's possible that Jesus expected it to be a permanent fixture in human society. . . . Letting the world know that Christ loves them through unity? Now that's a definition of church I think my generation can get behind.[4]

In the Lord I'll be ever thankful,
in the Lord I will rejoice!
Look to God, do not be afraid.
Lift up your voices, the Lord is near;
lift up your voices, the Lord is near.[5]

1 Moisés Silva, *Philippians*, 2005

2 Dietrich Bonhoeffer, *The Cost of Discipleship*, 1959

3 Earl F. Palmer, *Integrity*, 2000

4 Sarah Cunningham, *Dear Church*, 2006

5 Taizé Community, *In the Lord I'll Be Ever Thankful*

1. *How do you deal with disagreement? Where did you learn this behavior?*

2. *What could have happened in the Philippian church if the two women had not resolved their dispute?*

3. *What, for you, is the difference between "going to" church, "being part of" a church, and "being" church? Which description most accurately depicts your experience of contemporary Christ followers?*

4. *Do you agree with Moisés Silva that disputes between Christ followers cannot remain a personal thing? Why or why not?*

5. *What difference is there between arguments within the Church and arguments between a Christ follower and someone outside the Church?*

6. *Carefully reread the Sarah Cunningham quote. How would you describe the challenge this twenty-something woman is offering from the perspective of her disillusioned generation to individual Christ followers and to the Church as a whole?*

Therefore, my brothers and sisters . . . **stand firm in the Lord** *in this way, my beloved.*

Rachel Durfee, *Stand Firm*, 2000

Mala Sikka, *Touching Rocks*, 2004

1 Peter 2:5-6

. . . like living stones, let yourselves be built into a spiritual house, to be a holy priesthood, to offer spiritual sacrifices acceptable to God through Jesus Christ. For it stands in scripture: "See, I am laying in Zion a stone, a cornerstone chosen and precious; and whoever believes in him will not be put to shame."

Ephesians 2:19-22

So then you are no longer strangers and aliens, but you are citizens with the saints and also members of the household of God, built upon the foundation of the apostles and prophets, with Christ Jesus himself as the cornerstone. In him the whole structure is joined together and grows into a holy temple in the Lord; in whom you also are built together spiritually into a dwelling place for God.

Thanks be to you, Lord Jesus Christ:
in all my trials and sufferings
you have given me the strength to
    stand firm;
in your mercy you have granted me
a share of eternal glory.

Irenaeus of Sirmium (c. 120-c. 203)

Let us, then, hold steadfastly and unceasingly to our
Hope and to the Pledge of our righteousness, that is,
Christ Jesus, "who bore our sins in his own body on
the tree, who committed no sin, neither was guile
found on his lips"; but for our sakes he endured
everything that we might live in him. Therefore let us
be imitators of his patient endurance, and if we suffer
for the sake of his name, let us glorify him. For he set
us this example in his own Person, and this is what
we believed.

Polycarp, *The Letter of Saint Polycarp, Bishop of Smyrna, to the Philippians*,
early second century

My hope is built on nothing less
than Jesus' blood and righteousness.
I dare not trust the sweetest frame,
but wholly trust in Jesus' Name.

On Christ the solid Rock I stand;
all other ground is sinking sand,
all other ground is sinking sand.

When darkness seems to hide his face,
I rest on his unchanging grace.
In every high and stormy gale,
my anchor holds within the veil.

His oath, his covenant, his blood
support me in the whelming flood.
When all around my soul gives way,
he then is all my Hope and Stay.

When he shall come with trumpet sound,
O may I then in him be found.
Dressed in his righteousness alone,
faultless to stand before the throne.

Edward Mote, *My Hope Is Built on Nothing Less / The Solid Rock*, c.1834

O Prince of Life,
teach us to stand more boldly on your side,
to face the world and all our adversaries more courageously,
and not to let ourselves be dismayed by any storm of temptation;
may our eyes be steadfastly fixed on you in fearless faith;
may we trust you with perfect confidence
that you will keep us, save us, and bring us through
by the power of your grace and the riches of your mercy.

Gerhard Tersteegen (1697-1769), from *The Westminster Collection of Christian Prayers*

I urge Euodia and I urge Syntyche **to be of the same mind in the Lord**. *Yes, and I ask you also, my loyal companion, help these women . . .*

Karyn Percival, *Searching for the Peacemaker*

Paul is reminding us, "This is not the first time that Euodia and Syntyche have had their names said out loud in worship. I baptized you, Euodia. I baptized you, Syntyche. Your names are written in the book of life." He's not calling them down; he's calling them up to their baptismal identity. . . . Don't look at the damage, look at the image. Euodia, Syntyche, live together in the Lord. We know who you are; your names are written in the book of life.

Thomas G. Long, sermon excerpt, January 27, 2005

Refrain . . . from all anger, partiality, unjust judgment, keeping far from all love of money, not hastily believing evil of anyone, nor being severe in judgment, knowing that we all owe the debt of sin.

Polycarp, *The Letter of Saint Polycarp, Bishop of Smyrna, to the Philippians*, early second century

> Great God,
> as we are gathering,
> you watch your people come;
> as yet, we're walking out of step,
> help us to walk as one.
>
> Andrew Pratt, *Great God, as We Are Gathering*, stanza 1

Jesus, Lord, we look to thee;
let us in thy name agree;
show thyself the Prince of Peace,
bid our strife forever cease.

By thy reconciling love
every stumbling block remove;
each to each unite, endear;
come, and spread thy banner here.

Make us of one heart and mind,
gentle, courteous, and kind,
lowly, meek, in thought and word,
altogether like our Lord.

Let us for each other care,
each the other's burdens bear;
to thy church the pattern give,
show how true believers live.

Free from anger and from pride,
let us thus in God abide;
all the depths of love express,
all the heights of holiness.

Let us then with joy remove
to the family above;
on the wings of angels fly,
show how true believers die.

Charles Wesley, *Jesus, Lord, We Look to Thee*, 1749

Philippians 2:5

Let the same mind be in you that was in Christ Jesus. . . .

Exodus 36:2

Moses then called Bezalel and Oholiab and every skillful one to whom the LORD had given skill, everyone whose heart was stirred to come to do the work . . .

Deuteronomy 5:29

If only they had such a mind as this, to fear me and to keep all my commandments always, so that it might go well with them and with their children forever!

1 Kings 3:9

Give your servant therefore an understanding mind to govern your people, able to discern between good and evil; for who can govern this your great people?

1 Kings 10:24

People came from all over the world to be with Solomon and drink in the wisdom God had given him.

Eugene H. Peterson, *The Message*, 2002

Ezekiel 40:4

The man said to me, "Mortal, look closely and listen attentively, and set your mind upon all that I shall show you, for you were brought here in order that I might show it to you; declare all that you see to the house of Israel."

Daniel 10:12

He said to me, "Do not fear, Daniel, for from the first day that you set your mind to gain understanding and to humble yourself before your God, your words have been heard, and I have come because of your words.

Matthew 22:36-37

"Teacher, which commandment in the law is the greatest?" He said to him, "'You shall love the Lord your God with all your heart, and with all your soul, and with all your mind.'"

Romans 7:24b-25

Who will rescue me from this body of death? Thanks be to God through Jesus Christ our Lord! So then, with my mind I am a slave to the law of God, but with my flesh I am a slave to the law of sin.

1 Corinthians 1:10

Now I appeal to you, brothers and sisters, by the name of our Lord Jesus Christ, that all of you be in agreement and that there be no divisions among you, but that you be united in the same mind and the same purpose.

1 Corinthians 2:16

"For who has known the mind of the Lord so as to instruct him?" But we have the mind of Christ.

The Church is called to be a union of [those] with Christ in the love of the Father whereby their separate beings are made one with that perfect mutual interpenetration in love, that perfect community which is the glory of God. . . . The life of the Church is a real participation in the life of the triune God, wherein all life and all glory consist in self-giving. . . .

Lesslie Newbigin, *The Household of God*, 1953

May the grace of Christ, our Savior, and the Father's boundless love, with the Holy Spirit's favor, rest upon us from above. May we now remain in union with each other and the Lord, and possess, in sweet communion, joys that earth cannot afford.

John Newton, from *Olney Hymns*, 1779

Henri Matisse, *Dance I*, 1909

Matisse, Henri (1869-1954). Dance (I). Paris, Hôtel Biron, early 1909. Oil on canvas, 8' 6 1/2" x 12' 9 1/2" (259.7 x 390.1 cm). Gift of Nelson A. Rockefeller in honor of Alfred H. Barr, Jr. (201.1963). The Museum of Modern Art, New York, NY, U.S.A. © 2009 Succession H. Matisse / Artists Rights Society (ARS), New York. Digital Image © The Museum of Modern Art / Licensed by SCALA /Art Resource, NY.

Rejoice *in the Lord always; again I will say,* **Rejoice.** *Let your gentleness be known to everyone.* **The Lord is near.**

Martin Bulinya, *Untitled*

Joyful, joyful, we adore thee, God of glory, Lord of love.
Hearts unfold like flow'rs before thee, praising thee their sun above.
Melt the clouds of sin and sadness; drive the dark of doubt away.
Giver of immortal gladness, fill us with the light of day!

All thy works with joy surround thee, earth and heav'n reflect thy rays,
stars and angels sing around thee, center of unbroken praise.
Field and forest, vale and mountain, blooming meadow, flashing sea,
chanting bird and flowing fountain, call us to rejoice in thee.

Thou art giving and forgiving, ever blessing, ever bless'd,
well-spring of the joy of living, ocean-depth of happy rest!
Thou our Father, Christ our brother, all who live in love are thine.
Teach us how to love each other, lift us to the joy divine.

Mortals, join the mighty chorus which the morning stars began.
Love divine is reigning o'er us, leading us with mercy's hand.
Ever singing, march we onward, victors in the midst of strife.
Joyful music lifts us sunward in the triumph song of life!

Henry van Dyke, *Joyful, Joyful, We Adore Thee*, 1907, alt.

Clap hands, all lands,
our God acclaim!
With souls brimful of awe
come praise God's name!

God reigns, ordains,
sustains, empow'rs,
and grants this heritage:
that love is ours!

Horns sound! God crowned
with shouts now comes!
Let us with hymns praise God,
with skill sing psalms.

God's throne alone
shall be the place
where nations come to sing
in praise of grace.

So sing, and bring
all you create:
exalt the living God,
so good, so great!

John Core, *Clap Hands, All Lands*, 2005

Before the marvel of this night,
adoring, fold your wings and bow,
then tear the sky apart with light,
and with your news the world endow.
Proclaim the birth of Christ and peace,
that fear and death and sorrow cease:
sing peace, sing peace, sing Gift of Peace,
sing peace, sing Gift of Peace!

Awake the sleeping world with song,
this is the day the Lord has made.
Assemble here, celestial throng,
in royal splendor come arrayed.
Give earth a glimpse of heavenly bliss,
a teasing taste of what they miss.
Sing bliss, sing bliss, sing endless bliss,
sing bliss, sing endless bliss!

The love that we have always known,
our constant joy and endless light,
now to the loveless world be shown,
now break upon its deathly night.
Into one song compress the love
that rules our universe above:
sing love, sing love, sing God is love,
sing love, sing God is love!

Jaroslav J. Vajda, *Before the Marvel of This Night*

Always rejoicing, ceaselessly praying,
constantly thankful, voicing our praise;
sharing the joy that fathoms all grieving;
glad in the hope that lightens dark ways:

This is God's purpose, faith's expectation,
promised in Jesus, sealed by the cross:
joy that surpasses grief and elation:
hope that outreaches sorrow and loss.

Strong in the Spirit, facing earth's darkness,
we will inherit peace at God's side;
made, by Love's mercy, holy and blameless;
risen, rejoicing, with Christ who died.

Holy, Eternal, Love that creates us;
holy in Jesus, Love crucified;
holy as Spirit, Love that perfects us:
Love we adore you, Love glorified.

Alan Gaunt, *Always Rejoicing, Ceaselessly Praying*, 1989

Henri Matisse, *Maquette for Nuit de Noël*, 1952

Matisse, Henri (1869-1954). Maquette for Nuit de Noel. Nice-Cimiez, Hôtel Regina, early 1952. Gouache on cut-and-pasted paper, homasote panel, 10' 7" x 53 1/2" Gift of Time Inc. (421.1953.1-5). The Museum of Modern Art, New York, NY, U.S.A. © 2009 Succession H. Matisse / Artists Rights Society (ARS), New York. Digital Image © The Museum of Modern Art / Licensed by SCALA / Art Resource, NY.

Do not worry about anything, but in everything by prayer and supplication **with thanksgiving let your requests be made known** *to God.*

4:6

Almighty God, Father of all mercies,
we, your unworthy servants, give you humble thanks
for all your goodness and loving-kindness
to us and to all whom you have made.
We bless you for our creation, preservation,
and all the blessings of this life,
but above all for your immeasurable love
in the redemption of the world by our Lord Jesus Christ,
for the means of grace, and for the hope of glory.

And, we pray, give us such an awareness of your mercies
that with truly thankful hearts we may show forth your praise,
not only with our lips, but in our lives,
by giving up ourselves to your service,
and by walking before you
in holiness and righteousness all our days,
through Jesus Christ, our Lord,
to whom, with you and the Holy Spirit,
be honor and glory throughout all ages. Amen.

The Book of Common Prayer

Romans 8:26-27
Likewise the Spirit helps us in our weakness; for we do not know how to pray as we ought, but that very Spirit intercedes with sighs too deep for words. And God, who searches the heart, knows what is the mind of the Spirit, because the Spirit intercedes for the saints according to the will of God.

Behold another consolation, a medicine which healeth grief, and distress, and all that is painful. And what is this? Prayer, thanksgiving in all things. And so He wills that our prayers should not simply be requests, but thanksgivings too for what we have. For how should he ask for future things, who is not thankful for the past?

St. John Chrysostom (c. 347-407), *Homily XIV: Philippians iv:4-7*

Laura James, *Love One Another*, 2000

And **the peace of God**, *which surpasses all understanding*, **will guard your hearts** . . .

Vincent van Gogh, *The Good Samaritan (after Delacroix)*, 1890

Collection Kröller-Müller Museum, Otterlo, The Netherlands

Peace has come to mean the time when there aren't any wars or even when there aren't any major wars. Beggars can't be choosers; we'd most of us settle for that. But in Hebrew peace, *shalom*, means fullness, means having everything you need to be wholly and happily yourself.

One of the titles by which Jesus is known is Prince of Peace, and he used the word himself in what seem at first glance to be two radically contradictory utterances. On one occasion he said to the disciples, "Do not think that I have come to bring peace on earth; I have not come to bring peace, but a sword" (Matthew 10:34). And later on, the last time they ate together, he said to them, "Peace I leave with you; my peace I give to you" (John 14:27).

The contradiction is resolved when you realize that, for Jesus, peace seems to have meant not the absence of struggle, but the presence of love.

Frederick Buechner, *Beyond Words*, 2004

Come now, O Prince of Peace,
make us one body.
Come, O Lord Jesus;
reconcile your people.

Come now, O God of love,
make us one body.
Come, O Lord Jesus;
reconcile your people.

Come now and set us free,
O God our Savior.
Come, O Lord Jesus;
reconcile all nations.

Come, Hope of unity;
make us one body.
Come, O Lord Jesus;
reconcile all nations.

Geonyong Lee, Korea; para. Marion Pope, *Ososŏ / Come Now, O Prince of Peace*, 1988

The peace of mind that Christ can bring
is peace in knowing how to sing
in spite of doubts of why or how,
in spite of fears of here and now.

The peace that strengthens faithful souls
cannot be built on self-made goals,
but rather comes to those who heed
a call for help in time of need.

So one finds peace within the heart
when each with others bears a part.
When peace for me is peace for you,
then Christ is present, peace is true.

So Christ, invade our life and will
until we see your justice still
defining best all human worth,
reshaping dreams of peace on earth.

Jane Parker Huber, *The Peace of Mind That Christ Can Bring*, 1982

. . . the peace which is shalom is not merely the absence of hostility, not merely being in right relationship. Shalom at its highest is *enjoyment* in one's relationships. A nation may be at peace with all its neighbors and yet be miserable in its poverty. To dwell in shalom is to *enjoy* living before God, to *enjoy* living in one's physical surroundings, to *enjoy* living with one's fellows, to *enjoy* life with oneself.

Nicholas Wolterstorff, *Until Justice and Peace Embrace*, 1983

Psalm 91

Whoever feels at home in the presence of the
  Most Glorious God
shall be able to pass the night
in the shadow of the Almighty One,
for that person can say to the Lord God,
"My sanctuary! My Place-to-stand! My God in
  whom I am trusting!"

The Lord God shall extricate you from the trap
  of the Hunter!
God will save you from the sting of Death!
The Lord shall cover you with God's wings;
under God's wings you can run to hide.
Do not be afraid of midnight terror
or of sickness that stalks people in the daytime
or of pain that creeps up on one in the twilight
or of crippling disease that strikes while the sun
  shines:
a thousand may collapse right next to you,
ten thousand may be struck down; but you
  shall not perish—
God's truth shall protect you, fence you in,
while letting you see with your own eyes
how the godless are paid in full.

You have said, "The Lord God **is** my sanctuary!"
You have taken the Most Glorious God as your
  At-home!

Therefore Destruction cannot get you;
disaster shall never enter the door where you
  are living:
for God Almighty has made you a charge of
  God's angels,
ordering them to guard you in all that you do.
They shall hold you up by their hands
so that you do not even stub your foot against
  a stone,
so that you can walk past roaring lions and
  poisonous snakes,
so that you can step on and crush the lion and
  even . . .
the Dragon!

[Then God's voice itself ends the psalm]

"Because he or she has held fast to me, I shall
  save them!
Because she or he knows my name, I shall
  deliver them!
I will hear each one when that person cries out
  to me;
I will be with them in the terribly dark days,
free them from the Darkness, and bring them
  glory!
I will let him and her live peacefully on and on,
because I shall let them see my salvation!"

Calvin Seerveld, *Voicing God's Psalms*, 2005

Go in love,
for love endures forever.
Go in peace,
for it is the gift of God.
Go in safety,
for we cannot go where God is not.

Earle W. Fike, Jr., *Book of Worship*, 1964, alt.

Ann Boyer LePere, *Sheltered*, 2004

Focused Praise

Philippians 4:8-9

Philippians 4:8-9

. . . And the peace of God, which surpasses all understanding, will guard your hearts and your minds in Christ Jesus.

[8]Finally, beloved, whatever is true, whatever is honorable, whatever is just, whatever is pure, whatever is pleasing, whatever is commendable, if there is any excellence and if there is anything worthy of praise, think about these things. [9]Keep on doing the things that you have learned and received and heard and seen in me, and the God of peace will be with you.

I rejoice in the Lord greatly that now at last you have revived your concern for me; indeed, you were concerned for me, but had no opportunity to show it. . . .

In the final book of *The Lord of the Rings*, Sam Gamgee, an uncommonly courageous little Hobbit, wakes up following the climactic battle. Thinking everything is lost, and discovering instead that all his friends are around him, he cries out to Gandalf the great wizard: "I thought you were dead! But then I thought I was dead myself. Is everything sad going to come untrue?"[1]

Sooner or later, awakening to the truth of the Good News, every Christ follower will ask that same profoundly innocent question—"Is everything sad going to come untrue?" And because of the resurrection of Jesus Christ, God's answer will always be "Yes!"

But God's answer is God's promise—a promise that must initially be received by faith. Once received, however, God's emphatic "Yes!" to the pivotal question of our future forms our realization of how, and where, and to what extent God is at work.

God's "Yes!" is also our *only* source of hope. Hope itself is a gift from God. But the gift of hope is not an end in itself. Once received, God's gift of hope begins our spiritual transformation. Every Christ follower is being transformed by the power of the Holy Spirit, becoming an active participant—a partner in God's commitment to heal, restore, and redeem everything that has been diseased, disfigured, and destroyed: everything sad is coming untrue!

In another letter Paul wrote, "Do not be conformed to this world, but be transformed by the renewing of your minds, so that you may discern what is the will of God—what is good and acceptable and perfect."[2] Paul prefaced this challenge to nonconformity with other words: "I appeal to you therefore, brothers and sisters, by the mercies of God, to present your bodies as a living sacrifice, holy and acceptable to God, which is your spiritual worship."[3]

Writing about Paul, St. John Chrysostom said, "[Do you see,] that he desires to banish every evil thought from our souls; for evil actions spring from thoughts."[4] We underestimate the seductive power of evil if we presume that "evil thoughts" refer only to those "yearnings" we all share, and "evil actions" are the things we do when we act them out. Evil thoughts can include good intentions and evil actions can seem outwardly benevolent. The difference is in our focus.

Karl Barth described worldly focus well:

. . . [When human beings] will not live in the distinctive freedom of the man Jesus . . . [we are] therefore forced to regard [our] Fellow and Brother as a stranger and interloper, and his existence as an intolerable demand.

[We want] to be left alone by the God who has made this man a neighbor with his distinctive freedom . . . [We regard] the renewal of human nature declared in [Christ's] existence as quite unnecessary. [We see and feel,] perhaps, the [limitations and imperfections] of [our] present nature, but [these limitations] do not touch [us] so deeply that [we are] not finally satisfied with this nature and the way in which [we fulfill] it. A serious need, a hunger or thirst for [the renewal offered by Christ], is quite foreign to [us]. [We . . . see] no relevance in [this] man Jesus with his freedom to be a new [creation].

Again, [we think we have] a sober idea of what is attainable, of what is possible and impossible, within the limitations of [our] humanity. . . . The limited sphere with which [we are] content seems to [us] to be [our] necessary sphere, so that its transcendence in the freedom of the man Jesus is an imaginary work in which [we ourselves] can have no part.[5]

Is the Good News too good to be true? Have we become so blinded by the world that we believe we have no part in God's gift of hope? Do we perceive transformation—the renewing of our minds—as unnecessary?

Rejoice! The Lord is near!

God's peace will guard your hearts and minds in Christ Jesus.

Think on these things!

Paul's challenge to us is to be counter-cultural. In the context of post-modern culture, it is vitally important to imitate Paul's single-minded focus on Christ: the *nearness* of Christ, the *promise* of Christ, *comfort* in Christ, *hope* in Christ. Contemporary Christ followers can learn this discipline in every episode of *our* epic adventure. Then, even when we awaken from our greatest battles, we can look around in amazement and say to God, "I thought you were dead! But then I thought I was dead. . . . Is everything sad going to come untrue?"

"Yes!"

Now let our hearts be joyful, let earth the song begin,
let the whole world keep triumph, and all that is
*   therein.*
Let all things seen and unseen their notes of gladness
*   blend,*
for Christ the Lord is risen, our joy shall know no end. [6]

1 J. R. R. Tolkien, *The Return of the King*, 1955

2 Romans 12:2

3 Romans 12:1

4 St. John Chrysostom (c. 347-407), *Homily XIV: Philippians iv:4-7*

5 Karl Barth, *Church Dogmatics*, 1958

6 John of Damascus, *The Day of Resurrection*, 8th century; tr. John M. Neale, 1862, alt.

1. *What is "sad" in your life? If you knew, without a doubt, that everything sad was going to "come untrue," how would you respond? How, specifically, would that knowledge change the attitude and focus of your life?*

2. *Becky Pippert has suggested the greatest inhibitor to Christ followers sharing the Good News is an underlying skepticism that the Bible may not be true. How would you respond? What would it take to convince you of the absolute truth of Scripture?*

3. *What does Paul mean when he says, ". . . the Lord is near"? How does this reality impact your life, your faith, your joy?*

4. *When is the last time you truly rejoiced about anything, allowing joy to overwrite every other emotion and thought? What prompted such joy? How long did it last?*

5. *Karl Barth has articulated the essence of contemporary humanism. How do you respond to this quote? Does it frighten you, intrigue you, or describe you?*

6. *What would it take for you to develop a single-minded focus on Jesus Christ? How would you begin or continue that process? How does that connect with God's will for you?*

. . . **think about these things. Keep on doing the things** *that you have learned* . . .

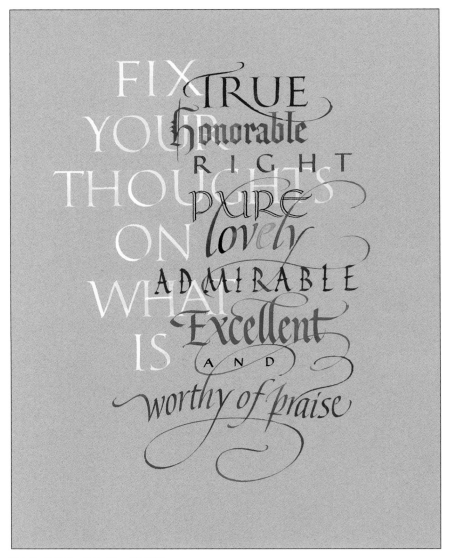

Timothy R. Botts, *Philippians 4:8*, 2000

Teach me, Lord Jesus, all I need to know:
form within me your mind;
let all the truth I find
make me more humble, more truly to grow.

Teach me, Lord Jesus, all I need to do:
help me by love to live,
suffer and work and give,
learning obedience, and learning from you.

Teach me, Lord Jesus, all I need to say:
set my tongue free to speak
true words, and pure and meek,
patterned on yours, which shall not pass away.

Teach me, Lord Jesus, all I need to be:
train me and put me right
till I reflect your light,
till you complete all your purpose for me.

Christopher M. Idle, *Teach Me, Lord Jesus, All I Need to Know*, 1981

Psalm 119:13-18
With my lips I declare
　　all the ordinances of your mouth.
I delight in the way of your decrees
　　as much as in all riches.
I will meditate on your precepts,
　　and fix my eyes on your ways.
I will delight in your statutes;
　　I will not forget your word.
Deal bountifully with your servant,
　　so that I may live and observe your word.
Open my eyes, so that I may behold
　　wondrous things out of your law.

[Things of beauty act as] an antidote against self-absorption, self-centeredness. Beauty takes the center *out of* self and places it elsewhere by demanding that we reckon with it, come to terms with it. That is art's saving grace. . . . Standing on beauty's threshold, however, we recognize that *beauty* is calling the shots, that *it* has summoned *us*—not vice versa.

Nathan D. Mitchell, "Being Beautiful, Being Just," essay from *Toward Ritual Transformation*, 2003

Psalm 92:12-15
The righteous flourish like the palm
    tree, and grow like a cedar in
    Lebanon.
They are planted in the house of the
    LORD; they flourish in the courts of
    our God.
In old age they still produce fruit; they
    are always green and full of sap,
showing that the LORD is upright;
    he is my rock, and there is no
    unrighteousness in him.

Cornelis Monsma, *Fruitful (Psalm 1:1-3)*, 2003

This painting depicts a gathering of Russian saints . . . There is no perspective to indicate space; it is a timeless gathering of human figures . . . Inspired by the Revelation of St. John . . . Kandinsky combined here the representation of saints and martyrs with the idea of Salvation. "Ascending with the rising sun" (which creeps up fiery red behind a kremlin), an angel blows a golden trumpet announcing the Redemption of the world through Jesus Christ. The dove of peace, carrying the olive twig to Noah's ark, symbolizes the Resurrection, as do the butterfly and the phoenix at the right. The dark sky at the upper right, with its almost black lunar eclipse and pale crescent, emphasizes the drama.

Hans K. Roethel, *Kandinsky*, 1979

Wassily Kandinsky, *Allerheiligen I (All Saints I)*, 1911

On Jordan's stormy banks I stand, and cast a wishful eye
to Canaan's fair and happy land, where my possessions lie.

I am bound for the Promised Land,
I am bound for the Promised Land.
Oh, who will come and go with me?
I am bound for the Promised Land.

There gen'rous fruits that never fail, on trees immortal grow.
There rocks and hills and brooks and vales with milk and honey flow.

All o'er those wide-extended plains shines one eternal day;
there God the Son forever reigns, and scatters night away.

No chilling winds or pois'nous breath can reach that healthful shore;
sickness and sorrow, pain and death are felt and feared no more.

When shall I reach that happy place and be forever blest?
When shall I see my Father's face, and in God's bosom rest?

Samuel Stennett, *I Am Bound for the Promised Land / On Jordan's Stormy Banks I Stand*, 1787

Psalm 85:6-11

Will you not revive us again,
   so that your people may rejoice in you?
Show us your steadfast love, O LORD,
   and grant us your salvation.

Let me hear what God the LORD will speak,
   for he will speak peace to his people,
      to his faithful, to those who turn to him in their hearts.
Surely his salvation is at hand for those who fear him,
   that his glory may dwell in our land.

Steadfast love and faithfulness will meet;
   righteousness and peace will kiss each other.
Faithfulness will spring up from the ground,
   and righteousness will look down from the sky.

what about justice
when you gotta make a choice
what will you say
when you gotta make it work
how will you act
when you gotta make it count
what will you do
when you know what Jesus would do

whatever is true
whatever is noble
whatever is right
whatever is pure
whatever is lovely
whatever is admirable
think about such things
and put it into practice
and the God of peace will be with you

glory to the Father
glory to the Son
glory to the Spirit
forever and ever
amen

Bennett P. Samuel, *what about justice*, 2008

Contentment

Philippians 4:10–20

Philippians 4:10-20

[10]I rejoice in the Lord greatly that now at last you have revived your concern for me; indeed, you were concerned for me, but had no opportunity to show it. [11]Not that I am referring to being in need; for I have learned to be content with whatever I have. [12]I know what it is to have little, and I know what it is to have plenty. In any and all circumstances I have learned the secret of being well-fed and of going hungry, of having plenty and of being in need. [13]I can do all things through him who strengthens me. [14]In any case, it was kind of you to share my distress.

[15]You Philippians indeed know that in the early days of the gospel, when I left Macedonia, no church shared with me in the matter of giving and receiving, except you alone. [16]For even when I was in Thessalonica, you sent me help for my needs more than once. [17]Not that I seek the gift, but I seek the profit that accumulates to your account. [18]I have been paid in full and have more than enough; I am fully satisfied, now that I have received from Epaphroditus the gifts you sent, a fragrant offering, a sacrifice acceptable and pleasing to God. [19]And my God will fully satisfy every need of yours according to his riches in glory in Christ Jesus. [20]To our God and Father be glory forever and ever. Amen.

*E*very human being is where we are and what we are because of other people. Paul wrote these words to another Christian community about the Christ followers in Philippi:

> . . . We want you to know about the grace that God has given the Macedonian churches. In the midst of a very severe trial, their overwhelming joy and their extreme poverty welled up in rich generosity. For I testify that they gave as much as they were able, and even beyond their ability. Entirely on their own, they urgently pleaded with us for the privilege of sharing in this service to the Lord's people. And they went beyond our expectations; having given themselves first of all to the Lord, they gave themselves by the will of God also to us.[1]

As Gordon Fee observed, "'affliction + poverty = abounding in generosity.' . . . Here [in Philippi] is a community where the gospel had done its certain work."[2] Paul was the beneficiary of the change the Good News had brought to Philippi. But the Philippian Christ followers received the ultimate blessing.

What can post-modern people learn from this first century commendation and the "thank you" note included in the text of Paul's Philippian letter? Contentment. Bill Hybels has said:

> There is a basic assumption that most of us have about material things: the more we have, the happier we will be. It is pretty common for us to think that more money will improve our quality of life. The more stuff we have, the more content we will be. Or so we think. . . . In all of this we have a deep inner sense that contentment is possible. It can be attained. We just are not sure exactly how to get there from here.[3]

Following a period of time when they could only *want* to support Paul in his ministry, the Philippian community was finally *able* to do so. Paul was overjoyed—but not for the gift as much as for the givers. Like a loving parent who can't say enough about a gift they really don't need—just because their child has had so much joy in giving it—Paul was profuse in his thanks to the devoted fellowship in Philippi, rejoicing with them, in Christ, at their ability to be generous. Through their generosity, they had experienced a form of spiritual resurrection—the budding of a tree branch that has shown great promise through the winter but is now in the full bloom of spring.

Paul also recognized a teachable moment. His joy was not dependent on his circumstances—the Philippians knew this. He could live with nothing or he could live with every desire fulfilled, and his joy was *exactly* the same.

In Christ, Paul was content, independent of the changing context of his life. Contentment was an attitude the Philippians were learning—relying on the same grace and peace Paul knew, doing all things in the name of the One who was their ultimate joy.

Christ-focused contentment is elusive today. "The very fact that you were able to purchase this book probably puts you among the world's wealthy."[4] But how many people reading these words are truly content?

Many people struggle with the power of money, thinking of their wealth either as an entitlement, a perk from God for faithful living, or as a neutral reality that can be used for good or for evil depending on intelligent discernment. Both views are contrary to Scripture. Frank Thielman once wrote, ". . . for the unbelieving world, money takes on a divine status. It is the god of this age, a god for which many are willing to sacrifice their happiness, their children, their health, indeed their own lives."[5] Christ followers share the same temptations.

The power of greed was not unknown to Paul. But Paul also knew the explosive power of greed could easily be defused through giving. As the twentieth century philosopher Jacques Ellul wrote, "There is one act par excellence which profanes money by going directly against the law of money, an act for which money is not made. This act is *giving*."[6]

Paul deeply appreciated the love the Philippian Christ followers showed in being his Christian family—literally *having community* with him in his troubles. This was nothing new among a devoted fellowship who loved each other deeply. But Paul's greater joy came with the knowledge that their faith was bearing fruit—that by

God's grace they were able to be increasingly generous with what little they actually had. Christ, not currency, had possession of their hearts—their true contentment.

For Paul, the uncommon generosity of the Philippians was positive proof of their ongoing growth into mature faith. This made their sacrificial offering for him pleasing—even fragrant—to God. As his offering in return, he reiterated his assurance that God, *in Jesus Christ*, would never fail to provide for them riches no amount of money could ever buy.

1 2 Corinthians 8:1-5 (TNIV)

2 Gordon D. Fee, *Paul's Letter to the Philippians*, 1995

3 Bill Hybels, *Run the Race*, 1999

4 Richard J. Foster, *Money, Sex & Power*, 1985

5 Frank Thielman, *Philippians*, 1995

6 Jacques Ellul, *Money and Power*, 1984

1. *Are you content? Why or why not?*

2. *If you had enough money to buy one amazing thing, what would you buy? How much money would it take? How would your life be different because you bought it?*

3. *If you had enough money to dramatically help one person, who would you help, and how much money would it take? How would your life be different because of your gift?*

4. *Which costs more—your answer to question 2 or your answer to question 3? Which answer comes closer to an expression of God's shalom?*

5. *When you set aside the money for your tithe or offering, is it one of the first things you do with your money or one of the last? Why?*

6. *How do your personal choices regarding money reflect or impact your contentment at the moment and your level of trust in God for the future?*

. . . **In any and all circumstances** *I have learned the secret* . . . *I can do all things* **through him** *who strengthens me.*

Vincent van Gogh,
The potato-eaters, 1885

Here, van Gogh tried to depict the spiritual quality of labor in the ritualistic sharing of a meal, under the light of a glowing lantern. . . . Van Gogh wrote that he had painted the figures in the dark colors of a "very dusty, unpeeled potato." The mood of the painting is deeply somber and the sharing of their meager repast suggests the sacred and solemn sharing of the sacramental elements of bread and wine in a eucharistic observance. . . . The potatoes . . . which resemble small, rounded loaves of bread passed from one individual to the next, recall the simple piety of the early Christians. . . . Their simple meal is an indirect reference to the presence of the divine, paralleling the overt reference of the somber crucifix hanging on the darkened wall.

Kathleen Powers Erickson, *At Eternity's Gate*, 1998

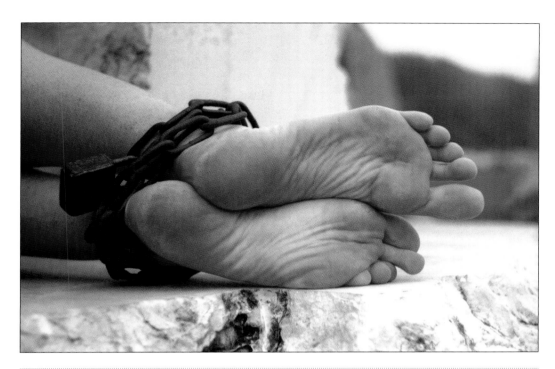

Dejan Novcic, *Ballerina's Soles*

People outside naturally find it difficult to imagine what prison life must be like. In itself, that is, each single moment, life here is not very different from anywhere else, so far. I spend my time reading, meditating, writing, pacing up and down my cell—without rubbing myself sore on the walls like a polar bear! The important thing is to make the best use of one's possessions and capabilities—there are still plenty left—and to accept the limits of the situation, by which I mean not giving way to feelings of resentment and discontent. I have never realized so clearly what the Bible and Luther mean by spiritual trial. Quite suddenly, for no apparent reason, whether physical or psychological, the peace and placidity which have been a mainstay hitherto begin to waver, and the heart, in Jeremiah's expressive phrase, becomes that defiant and despondent thing one cannot fathom. It is like an invasion from outside, as though evil powers were trying to deprive one of life's dearest treasures. But it is a wholesome and necessary experience which helps one to a better understanding of human life.

Dietrich Bonhoeffer, from "A Wedding Sermon from a Prison Cell, May 1943"

Pray for the church in Syria, [from which] I am being sent off to Rome as a prisoner. I am the least of the faithful there—yet I have been privileged to serve God's honor.

Ignatius, *The Letters of Ignatius, Bishop of Antioch, To the Ephesians*, c. A.D. 100

As the feast of God's people here and now, the Eucharist reminds us that one day we will all sit at God's great "welcome table" and pass the food until all are filled. When the Holy Spirit enlivens our meals, we share in this abundant feast even now.

Martha L. Moore-Keish, from *A More Profound Alleluia*, 2004

Before you, Lord, who can pretend
to more than mind can comprehend?
Who dares to pray with prideful stare,
with selfish heart, or haughty air?

*O people chosen, called, and blessed,
wait for the Lord and trusting rest
where hope grows strong and cares decrease:
the calm, still center of God's peace.*

Save us, O God, from frantic hearts;
unleash our lives from greed's grim arts;
reform us from our envious bent,
and teach our souls to be content. *Refrain*

Held like a child serene and sure
who on its mother rests secure,
may we rely on you alone
and know our life to be your own. *Refrain*

Carl P. Daw, Jr., *Before You, Lord, Who Can Pretend? (Psalm 131)*, 2001

Now Christ is the only food of our soul, and therefore our Heavenly Father invites us to Christ, that, refreshed by partaking of him, we may repeatedly gather strength until we shall have reached heavenly immortality.

John Calvin, *Institutes of the Christian Religion*, 1536

(And I shall know exactly what happened
  Today between noon and three)
That we, too, may come to the picnic
  With nothing to hide, join the dance
As it moves in perichoresis,
  Turns about the abiding tree.

W. H. Auden (1907-1973), excerpt, "Compline," from "Horae Canonicae,"
Selected Poetry of W. H. Auden

Psalm 131

O LORD, my heart is not lifted up,
  my eyes are not raised too high;
I do not occupy myself with things
  too great and too marvelous for me.
But I have calmed and quieted my soul,
like a weaned child with its mother;
  my soul is like the weaned child that
    is with me.
O Israel, hope in the LORD
  from this time on and forevermore.

Philippians 4:13
I can do all things through him who strengthens me.

Philippians 2:12b-13a
. . . work out your own salvation with fear and trembling; for it is God who is at work in you. . . .

Romans 8:26
. . . the Spirit helps us in our weakness; for we do not know how to pray as we ought, but that very Spirit intercedes with sighs too deep for words.

*I sought the Lord, and afterward I knew
he moved my soul to seek him, seeking me;
it was not I that found, O Savior true;
no, I was found, was found of thee.*

Anonymous, *I Sought the Lord, and Afterward I Knew*, 1878

Watanabe Sadao, *The Last Supper*, 1981

Psalm 141

I call upon you, O Lord; come quickly to me;
  give ear to my voice when I call to you.
Let my prayer be counted as incense before you,
  and the lifting up of my hands as an evening sacrifice.

Set a guard over my mouth, O Lord;
  keep watch over the door of my lips.
Do not turn my heart to any evil,
  to busy myself with wicked deeds
in company with those who work iniquity;
  do not let me eat of their delicacies.

Let the righteous strike me;
  let the faithful correct me.
Never let the oil of the wicked anoint my head,
  for my prayer is continually against their wicked deeds.
When they are given over to those who shall condemn them,
  then they shall learn that my words were pleasant.
Like a rock that one breaks apart and shatters on the land,
  so shall their bones be strewn at the mouth of Sheol.

But my eyes are turned toward you, O God, my Lord;
  in you I seek refuge; do not leave me defenseless.
Keep me from the trap that they have laid for me,
  and from the snares of evildoers.
Let the wicked fall into their own nets,
  while I alone escape.

Hebrews 13:15

Through Jesus, therefore, let us continually offer to God a sacrifice of praise—the fruit of lips that confess his name. *NIV*

Vitali Komarov, *Peach Tree Orchard*, 2001

Leviticus 7:11-12
These are the instructions for the
Peace-Offering which is presented
to God. If you bring it to offer
thanksgiving, then along with the
Thanksgiving-Offering present
unraised loaves of bread mixed with
oil, unraised wafers spread with oil,
and cakes of fine flour, well-kneaded
and mixed with oil. . . .

Eugene H. Peterson, *The Message*, 2002

Annie Vallotton, *The Woman Anointing Jesus' Feet*, 1976

Luke 7:44-46
Then turning toward the woman, he said to Simon, "Do you see this woman? I entered your house; you gave me no water for my feet, but she has bathed my feet with her tears and dried them with her hair. You gave me no kiss, but from the time I came in she has not stopped kissing my feet. You did not anoint my head with oil, but she has anointed my feet with ointment. . . ."

Bring we the frankincense of our love
to the feet of the holy Child,
ever remembering God's great gift
of a life that is undefiled.

Bring we the myrrh of humility
to the throne of the Son of God,
ever recalling the purity
of his life when the earth he trod.

Ever secure in his changelessness,
though the kingdoms of earth may fall,
bring we the gold of our faithfulness
to the King who is Lord of all.

H. Kenn Carmichael, *Bring We the Frankincense of Our Love*, 1976

Then with good and just cause, we offer and submit ourselves completely to God the Father and to our Lord Jesus Christ, in recognition of so many and so great benefits. And (as Christian love requires) we testify this by holy offerings and gifts which are administered to Jesus Christ in His least ones, to those who are hungry, thirsty, naked, strangers, sick, or held in prison. For all who live in Christ, and have Him dwelling them [sic], do voluntarily what the law commands them. And the latter commands that one not appear before God without an offering.

John Calvin, *La forme des prieres*

Psalm 116:12-19

What shall I return to the LORD
　for all his bounty to me?
I will lift up the cup of salvation
　and call on the name of the LORD,
I will pay my vows to the LORD
　in the presence of all his people.
Precious in the sight of the LORD
　is the death of his faithful ones.
O LORD, I am your servant;
　I am your servant, the child of your serving girl.
　You have loosed my bonds.
I will offer to you a thanksgiving sacrifice
　and call on the name of the LORD.
I will pay my vows to the LORD
　in the presence of all his people,
in the courts of the house of the LORD,
　in your midst, O Jerusalem.
Praise the LORD!

God, whose giving knows no ending, from your rich and endless store,
nature's wonder, Jesus' wisdom, costly cross, grave's shattered door:
Gifted by you, we turn to you, off'ring up ourselves in praise;
thankful song shall rise forever, gracious donor of our days.

Skills and time are ours for pressing toward the goals of Christ, your Son:
all at peace in health and freedom, races joined, the Church made one.
Now direct our daily labor, lest we strive for self alone;
born with talents, make us servants fit to answer at your throne.

Treasure too you have entrusted, gain through pow'rs your grace conferred;
ours to use for home and kindred, and to spread the gospel Word.
Open wide our hands, in sharing, as we heed Christ's ageless call,
healing, teaching, and reclaiming, serving you by loving all.

Robert L. Edwards, *God, Whose Giving Knows No Ending*, 1961

Cullen Washington, *Praising*, 2003

*And **my God will fully satisfy every need** of yours according to his riches in glory in Christ Jesus. . . .*

Reap me the earth as a harvest for God,
gather and bring it again,
all that is his, to the Maker of all;
lift it and offer it high.

> *Bring bread, bring wine, give glory to the Lord;*
> *whose is the earth but God's,*
> *whose is the praise but his?*

Go with your song and your music, with joy,
go to the altar of God;
carry your offerings, fruits of the earth,
work of your laboring hands. *Refrain*

Gladness, and pity, and passion, and pain,
all that is ours and must die—
lay all before him, return him his gift,
God, to whom all shall go home: *Refrain*

Luke Connaughton, *Reap Me the Earth as a Harvest for God*, alt.
© McCrimmons

The holy gifts of G
prepared from grap
are offered, blessed,
when Christian peo

In peace, we gather
our purpose makes
in Eucharistic bread
we meet God's only

His promises we cla
that Christ in us wi
and we in him, abid
in this great myster

We take and eat and
upon our Savior fee
our thankful hearts
as he accepts our ne

Thus, strengthened
unearned and undes
God sends us forth,
in others may be se

Rae E. Whitney, *The Holy Gif*

Joan Bohlig, *On the Table, Fruit*, 2005

For your generous providing
which sustains us all our days,
for your Spirit here residing,
we proclaim our heartfelt praise.
Through the depths of joy and sorrow,
though the road be smooth or rough,
fearless, we can face tomorrow
for your grace will be enough.

Hush our world's seductive voices
tempting us to stand alone;
save us from the siren voices
calling us to trust our own.
For those snared by earthly treasure,
lured by false security,
Jesus, true and only measure,
spring the trap to set folk free.

Round your table, through your giving,
show us how to live and pray
till your kingdom's way of living
is the bread we share each day:
bread for us and for our neighbor,
bread for body, mind, and soul,
bread of heaven and human labor—
broken bread that makes us whole.

Leith Fisher (1941-2009), *For Your Generous Providing*

Psalm 146
Hallelujah!

Praise the Lord, my heart!
My whole life, give praise.
Let me sing to God
as long as I live.

Never depend on rulers:
born of earth, they cannot save.
They die, they turn to dust.
That day, their plans crumble.

They are wise who depend on God,
who look to Jacob's Lord,
creator of heaven and earth,
maker of the teeming sea.

The Lord keeps faith for ever,
giving food to the hungry,
justice to the poor,
freedom to captives.

The Lord opens blind eyes
and straightens the bent,
comforting widows and orphans,
protecting the stranger.
The Lord loves the just
but blocks the path of the wicked.

Zion, praise the Lord!
Your God reigns for ever,
from generation to generation.
Hallelujah!

The Psalter

Banquet Scene, Catacomb of St. Callixtus, Rome, Italy, first half 3rd century

Blessed are those who put their trust in you, O God,
our sure rock and refuge.
Guard us from giving to any other
the allegiance which only belongs to you.
Shine upon us with the brightness of your light,
that we may love you with a pure heart
and praise you forever;
through Jesus Christ our Lord. **Amen.**

Lutheran Book of Worship: Minister's Desk Edition, 1978

Grace and Peace

Philippians 4:21–23

Philippians 4:21-23

. . . To our God and Father be glory forever and ever. Amen.

[21]Greet every saint in Christ Jesus. The friends who are with me greet you. [22]All the saints greet you, especially those of the emperor's household.

[23]The grace of the Lord Jesus Christ be with your spirit.

As Paul began his letter, so he now ends it, with greetings and the promise of God's grace. Everyone sends their greetings—all the friends of Paul in Christ, and all the "saints." To be a saint is to share fellowship with Jesus. To be in a community of saints is, as we have seen many times throughout this letter, to be mutually dependent and mutually dependable—not relying on the strength of the commitment we make to one another, but on the covenant commitment we share with God in Jesus Christ.

And look who's part of God's covenant! Not only the predictable Christ followers in Rome, but also members of the imperial house staff whom Paul has either met or converted! The Good News that spread throughout Rome continues to be shared today.

Paul closes his letter with echoes of his greeting.

Grace—in the Lord Jesus Christ. May this grace be the cherished position of every Christ follower until the Kingdom comes, and may it be our greatest joy to share Christ with one another in our devoted fellowship and, most especially, with an unbelieving world.

> On our way rejoicing gladly let us go.
> Christ our Lord has conquered; vanquished is the foe.
> Christ without, our safety; Christ within, our joy;
> who, if we be faithful, can our hope destroy?
>
> Unto God the Father joyful songs we sing;
> unto God the Savior thankful hearts we bring;
> unto God the Spirit bow we and adore,
> on our way rejoicing now and evermore![1]

1 John S. B. Monsell, *On Our Way Rejoicing*, 1863, rev. 1873

1. What do you think of when you hear the word "saint"? How does it make you feel to be called a "saint"?

2. What specific difference does it make if our faith is based on the commitment we make to love and serve God or if our faith relies on the commitment God has made to us in the life, death, and resurrection of Jesus Christ?

3. Who in your life needs to know the Good News about Jesus Christ? How can God use you to share the truth of God's love for them? Does imitating Christ-like humility play a part?

4. At the end of this book, how would you define God's shalom? What importance does that have in your life?

5. How would you define agape? How does this understanding define you?

6. How would you define joy? What is God leading you to do about it?

Icon of SS Peter and Paul

Then the Deacon cries aloud, "Receive one another; and let us kiss one another." Think not that this kiss is of the same character with those given in public by common friends. It is not such: but this kiss blends souls one with another, and courts entire forgiveness for them. The kiss therefore is the sign that our souls are mingled together, and banish all remembrance of wrongs. For this cause Christ said, If you are offering your gift at the altar, and there remember that your brother has anything against time, leave there your gift upon the altar, and go your way; first be reconciled to your brother, and then come and offer your gift. The kiss therefore is reconciliation, and for this reason holy: as the blessed Paul somewhere cried, saying, Greet ye one another with a holy kiss; and Peter, with a kiss of charity.

Cyril of Jerusalem (c. 313-386), from *Catechetical Lecture 23*

Psalm 85:10
Steadfast love and faithfulness will meet;
righteousness and peace will kiss each other.

Amanda Patrick, *Peace on Earth*, 2005

Lord, dismiss us with your blessing;
fill our hearts with joy and peace.
Let us each, your love possessing,
triumph in redeeming grace.
O direct us and protect us
traveling through this wilderness.

Thanks we give and adoration
for your gospel's joyful sound.
May the fruits of your salvation
in our hearts and lives abound.
Ever faithful, ever faithful
to your truth may we be found.

attr. John Fawcett, *Lord, Dismiss Us with Your Blessing*, 1773

Anneke Kaai, *Grace*, 2003

God has accepted your offering in
    Christ;
go now to offer yourselves,
as God's people,
to the world God loves;
and the blessing of God,
Father, Son, and Holy Spirit,
be with you all.

Prayers for Contemporary Worship

Amen.

So let it be.

Text Sources

(in order of appearance)

Introduction

Donald Elliott, from *The Westminster Collection of Christian Prayer*, © Donald Elliott

Hans R. Rookmaaker, *The Complete Works of Hans R. Rookmaaker*, vol. 4: *Western Art and the Meanderings of a Culture*, ed. Marleen Hengelaar-Rookmaaker (Carlisle, UK: Piquant, 2002), 234

Moisés Silva, *Philippians*, 2nd ed. (Baker Exegetical Commentary on the New Testament), ed. Robert Yarbrough and Robert H. Stein (Grand Rapids, MI: Baker Academic, 2005), 4

Chaido Koukouli-Chrysantaki, in *Philippi at the Time of Paul and after His Death*, ed. Charalambos Bakirtzis and Helmut Koester (Harrisburg, PA: Trinity Press International, 1998), 16-17

Chaido Koukouli-Chrysantaki, in *Philippi at the Time of Paul and after His Death*, ed. Charalambos Bakirtzis and Helmut Koester (Harrisburg, PA: Trinity Press International, 1998), 20-21

William Barclay, *The Letters to the Philippians, Colossians, and Thessalonians*, rev. ed., The Daily Study Bible Series (Philadelphia: Westminster Press, 1975), 3

This Is the Threefold Truth. Words: Fred Pratt Green. © 1980 Hope Publishing Company, Carol Stream, IL 60188. All rights reserved. Used by permission.

Bruce L. McCormack, introductory essay from Karl Barth, *The Epistle to the Philippians*, tr. James W. Leitch, 40th Anniversary Edition (Louisville and London: Westminster John Knox Press, 2002), xxiii

Richard Sibbes, from Selina F. Fox, *A Chain of Prayer across the Ages* (New York: E. P. Dutton & Co., 1943), 151

1:1-2 Grace and Peace

1:1a

William Barclay, *The Letters to the Philippians, Colossians, and Thessalonians*, rev. ed. (Philadelphia: Westminster Press, 1975), 9

Thomas G. Long, "Saints" (sermon on 1 Cor. 1), 1996

Preachers of the God of Grace. Words: Christopher M. Idle. © 1976 The Jubilate Group (admin. Hope Publishing Company, Carol Stream, IL 60188). All rights reserved. Used by permission.

1:1b

Augustine, excerpt from the English translation of *The Liturgy of the Hours* © 1974, International Committee on English in the Liturgy, Inc. All rights reserved.

For All the Saints Who Showed Your Love. John L. Bell. Copyright © 1989, 1996, Wild Goose Resource Group, Iona Community, Scotland. GIA Publications, Inc., exclusive North American agent, 7404 S. Mason Ave., Chicago, IL 60638 (www.giamusic. com; 800.442.1358). All rights reserved. Used by permission.

Thomas G. Long, "Saints" (sermon on 1 Cor. 1), 1996

Karl Barth, *The Epistle to the Philippians*, tr. James W. Leitch, 40th Anniversary Edition (Louisville and London: Westminster John Knox Press, 2002), 10

G. K. Beale, *The Temple and the Church's Mission: A Biblical Theology of the Dwelling Place of God*, New Studies in Biblical Theology 17, ed. D. A. Carson (Downers Grove, IL: InterVarsity Press; Leicester, UK: Apollos, 2004), 402

Thomas G. Long, "Accompany Them with Singing: The Recovery of Authentic Christian Funeral Practices," 2007, www.calvin.edu/worship/services/occasion/funerals/accompany_singing.php

Maya Angelou, excerpt, "Just Like Job," from *The Complete Collected Poems of Maya Angelou* (New York: Random House, 1994), 173

Scott Mutter, *Surrational Images: Photomontages* (Urbana and Chicago: University of Illinois Press, 1992), #21

1:2

Iona Community, from David Adam, *The Edge of Glory: Prayers in the Celtic Tradition* (Wilton, CT: Morehouse-Barlow, 1985), 91

The Psalter: A Faithful and Inclusive Rendering from the Hebrew into Contemporary English Poetry, Intended Primarily for Communal Song and Recitation, ed. Gabe Huck (Chicago: Liturgy Training Publications, 1995)

Scott Hoezee, *The Riddle of Grace: Applying Grace to the Christian Life* (Grand Rapids, MI, and Cambridge, UK: Wm. B. Eerdmans Publishing Company, 1996), 22

Charles Wesley, *Thou Hidden Source of Calm Repose*, 1749. Public domain.

Matthew Henry's Concise Commentary on the Bible [Rev. 1:4-8] (Nashville: Thomas Nelson, 1997)

Anneke Kaai and Eugene H. Peterson, *In a Word: See What You Believe* (Brewster, MA: Paraclete Press, and Carlisle, UK: Piquant, 2003), 59

1:3-11 Confident Prayer

section intro. text

C. S. Lewis, *The Chronicles of Narnia: The Horse and His Boy* (New York: HarperCollins Publishers, 1954), 162-63

Ruth Haley Barton, *Sacred Rhythms: Arranging Our Lives for Spiritual Transformation* (Downers Grove, IL: InterVarsity Press, 2006), 116-19

1:3-5

The Heidelberg Catechism, Q&A 55, alt. www.ccel.org/creeds/heidelberg-cat.html

Polycarp, *The Letter of Saint Polycarp, Bishop of Smyrna, to the Philippians*, from *The Library of Christian Classics*, vol. I: *Early Christian Fathers*, ed. Cyril C. Richardson (Philadelphia: Westminster Press, and London: S.C.M. Press, Ltd., 1953), 131

Mary Nelson Keithahn, *Sing Praise for the Journey*, 2000 © 2003 Zimbel Press, www.zimbel.com

World Council of Churches, *Jesus Christ the Life of the World: A Worship Book for the Sixth Assembly of the World Council of Churches* (Geneva: World Council of Churches, 1983), 49-50 [21] © 1983, World Council of Churches. Used by permission.

1:6

Augustus M. Toplady, *A Debtor to Mercy Alone*, 1771. Public domain.

Kenneth Koeman, "There are many times . . . ," *Reformed Worship* 27 (March 1993): 41. Copyright © 1993 Faith Alive Christian Resources. Used by permission.

1:7-8

John I. Durham, *The Biblical Rembrandt: Human Painter in a Landscape of Faith* (Macon, GA: Mercer University Press, 2004), 29-30

St. John Chrysostom, *Homily on Philippians ii.1.7*

Terry Waite, from *Prayers Encircling the World: An International Anthology of 300 Contemporary Prayers* (Great Britain: SPCK, 1998; Louisville: Westminster John Knox Press, 1999), 87 #94 © SPCK/Triangle, Holy Trinity Church, Marylebone Road, London NW1 4DU. Used by permission of SPCK and Westminster John Knox Press.

Søren Kierkegaard, translated in *Selected Readings*, edited by Robert Van de Weyer (Hunt & Thorpe, 1991). Used by permission.

We Are the Singers. Words: Shirley Erena Murray. © 1996 Hope Publishing Company, Carol Stream, IL 60188. All rights reserved. Used by permission.

1:9-10a

Book of Common Order of the Church of Scotland (Edinburgh: Saint Andrew Press, 1994), 13. © 1994 Panel on Worship of the Church of Scotland. Used by permission.

Augustine, *The Writings against the Manicheans, and against the Donatists*, from *A Select Library of the Christian Church: Nicene and Post-Nicene Fathers* (First Series), vol. 4, ed. Philip Schaff (Peabody, MA: Hendrickson Publishers, Inc., 1995, 2nd ed.; reprint ed. from Christian Literature Publishing Company, 1887), 48

John D. Witvliet, *Worship Seeking Understanding: Windows into Christian Practice* (Grand Rapids, MI: Baker Academic, 1993), 269

Paul Detterman, 2005. Public domain. Phil. 1:9-11 (NIV)

1:10b-11

Philip D. Kenneson, *Life on the Vine: Cultivating the Fruit of the Spirit in Christian Community* (Downers Grove, IL: InterVarsity Press, 1999), 18–19

Speak, O Lord. Keith Getty / Stuart Townend. © 2006 Thankyou Music (admin. by EMI Christian Music Publishing). All rights reserved. Used by permission.

Wesley, John, *Explanatory Notes Upon the New Testament* (J. Soule and T. Mason, for the Methodist Episcopal Church in the United States, 4th American Edition, 1818; 1st ed. 1755), 522–23

1:11

Frances Ridley Havergal, "Afterwards," from *The Poetical Works of Frances Ridley Havergal*, comp. Frances Anna Shaw and Maria Vernon Graham Havergal (New York: E. P. Dutton and Co., 1889), 335–36

1:12-21 Divine Purpose

section intro. text

Maxie D. Dunnam, *The Preacher's Commentary Series*, vol. 31: *Galatians, Ephesians, Philippians, Colossians, Philemon* (Nashville: Thomas Nelson Publishers, 1982), 262-63

1:12-14

When Prison Walls Extend Their Reach. Words: Christopher M. Idle. © 1993 The Jubilate Group (admin. Hope Publishing Company, Carol Stream, IL 60188). All rights reserved. Used by permission.

Ignatius Loyola, from *2000 Years of Prayer*, comp. Michael Counsell (Harrisburg, PA: Morehouse Publishing, 1999), 203-4

Edicio de la Torre, Philippines, "Prayer for Our Times," 1984, from *Touching Ground, Taking Root: Theological and Political Reflections on the Philippine Struggle* (London: Catholic Institute for International Relations [CIIP], in association with the British Council of Churches, 1986), 176. Copyright ©1986 Socio-Pastoral Institute (SPI), Manila.

Troy Rienstra, "The Church Behind Bars: A Prisoner's Plea to Christians on the Outside," from *The Banner* (Grand Rapids, MI: Faith Alive Christian Resources), Sept. 2005, 19

J. H. Oldham, from *The Communion of Saints: Prayers of the Famous*, ed. Horton Davies (Grand Rapids, MI: Wm. B. Eerdmans Publishing Company, 1990), 77

Martin Luther King, Jr., "Letter from a Birmingham Jail," April 16, 1963. www.africa.upenn.edu/Articles_Gen/Letter_Birmingham.html

Be Ye Glad. Michael Kelly Blanchard. © 1980 New Spring Publishing, Inc. /Paragon Music (ASCAP) (Administered by Brentwood-Benson Music Publishing, Inc.) / Gotz Music (ASCAP)

Be Ye Glad. Michael Kelly Blanchard. © 1980 Gotz Music (Administered by The Copyright Company, Nashville, TN) Diadem Sky / Paragon Music Corp. All rights reserved. International copyright secured. Used by permission.

1:15-18a

Blaise Pascal, from *2000 Years of Prayer*, comp. Michael Counsell (Harrisburg, PA: Morehouse Publishing, 1999), 286

Sing of Foolishness and Wisdom. Text: Richard Leach, 2005. Text © 2005 Selah Publishing Co., Inc. www.selahpub.com. All rights reserved. Used by permission.

Bryan Hiott, 1999, The Episcopal Church and Visual Arts, online exhibit, www.ecva.org/exhibition/light/pages/hiott.html

1:18b-19

Charles Wesley, *Come, Thou Long-Expected Jesus*, 1744. Public domain.

Isaac Watts, *O Bless the Lord, My Soul!* (after Psalm 103), 1719. Public domain.

1:20

Lord, Bless Your Church. Text: David A. Robb, 1991. Text © 2000 Selah Publishing Co., Inc. www.selahpub.com. All rights reserved. Used by permission.

1:21

Ki-Chul Joo, Korea, from *I Will Offer My Blood*, 1968, tr. Eugene Eung-Chun Park. Used by permission of Eugene Eung-Chun Park.

Ignatius, *The Letters of Ignatius, Bishop of Antioch: To the Romans*, from *The Library of Christian Classics*, vol. I: *Early Christian Fathers*, ed. Cyril C. Richardson (Philadelphia: Westminster Press, and London: S.C.M. Press, Ltd., 1953), 103-4

1:22-30 Standing Firm

section intro. text

1:22-24

The Belgic Confession, excerpt from Article 24, from *The Psalter Hymnal* (Grand Rapids, MI: CRC Publications, 1987), 841

1:25-26

1:27-30

Jeremy Taylor, from *2000 Years of Prayer*, comp. Michael Counsell (Harrisburg, PA: Morehouse Publishing, 1999), 278

Crosswinds, England, from *Prayers Encircling the World: An International Anthology of 300 Contemporary Prayers* (Great Britain: SPCK, 1998; Louisville: Westminster John Knox Press, 1999), 154 #192. Used by permission of Crosswinds, PO Box 1041, Nailsea, Somerset, BS19 2SD.

This Is My One, My Lifelong Wish / Nae pyŏngsaeng sowŏn. Anonymous, Korea; para. Marion Kim. Copyright © 1990, 2000, Christian Conference of Asia, admin. GIA Publications, Inc., 7404 S. Mason Ave., Chicago, IL 60638 (www.giamusic.com; 800.442.1358). All rights reserved. Used by permission.

George F. MacLeod, excerpt, "An Earth Redeemed," from *The Whole Earth Shall Cry Glory: Iona Prayers by Rev. George F. MacLeod*, 2nd ed. (Glasgow: Wild Goose Publications, 2007), 48. © The Iona Community. Used with permission.

2:1-4 Finding One Mind

section intro. text

Dietrich Bonhoeffer, *The Cost of Discipleship*, 2nd ed., tr. R. H. Fuller, rev. Irmgard Booth (New York: Macmillan Company, 1959), 45

Tod E. Bolsinger, *It Takes a Church to Raise a Christian: How the Community of God Transforms Lives* (Grand Rapids, MI: Brazos Press, 2004), 72

John Calvin, *Institutes of the Christian Religion*, ed. John T. McNeill, tr. Ford Lewis Battles (Philadelphia: Westminster Press, 1960), 4.2.5, 1047

C. S. Lewis, *Mere Christianity*, rev. and ampl. ed. (London: Geoffrey Bles, 1952), 101

2:1

Fred B. Craddock, *Philippians*, from *Interpretation: A Bible Commentary for Teaching and Preaching*, ed. James Luther Mays (Atlanta: John Knox Press, 1985), 35

David A. Davis, "The Shepherd's Voice," 2006 (sermon on John 10:1-8, May 7, 2006, Nassau Presbyterian Church), www.nassauchurch.org/worship/sermons/20060507.htm

2:2a

Reinhold Niebuhr, *Hymns for Worship*, *prepared for the Council of North American Student Christian Movements of the World's Student Christian Federation*, ed. Ursula Niebuhr (New York: Association Press, 1939), 241. Used by permission of Christopher Niebuhr.

Søren Kierkegaard, *Training in Christianity*, tr. Walter Lowrie (Princeton: Princeton University Press, 1944), 227. Reprinted by permission of Princeton University Press.

Ignatius, *The Letters of Ignatius*, *Bishop of Antioch: To the Ephesians*, from *The Library of Christian Classics*, vol. I: *Early Christian Fathers*, ed. Cyril C. Richardson (Philadelphia: Westminster Press, and London: S.C.M. Press, Ltd., 1953), 88

Lord, Help Us Walk Your Servant Way. Herman G. Stuempfle, Jr. Copyright © 1997 by GIA Publications, Inc., 7404 S. Mason Ave., Chicago, IL 60638 (www. giamusic.com; 800.442.1358). All rights reserved. Used by permission.

2:5-11 Imitating Christ
section intro. text

Earl F. Palmer, *Integrity: A Commentary on the Book of Philippians* (Vancouver, CA: Regent College Publishing, 2000; orig. ed. InterVarsity Press, 1992, as *Integrity in a World of Pretense: Insights from the Book of Philippians*), 93

James Montgomery Boice, *Philippians: An Expositional Commentary* (Grand Rapids, MI: Zondervan Publishing House, 1971), 126

Tom Wright, *Paul for Everyone: The Prison Letters: Ephesians, Philippians, Colossians and Philemon*, 2d ed. (London: SPCK, and Louisville, KY: Westminster John Knox Press, 2004), 103-4

Charles Wesley, *And Can It Be*, 1738. Public domain.

The Joyful Exchange. Gracia Grindal, 2005. © 2006 Wayne Leupold Editions, Inc. Used by permission. www. wayneleupold.com

attr. Amy Carmichael. Public domain.

One with God before Creation. Herman G. Stuempfle, Jr. Copyright © 2000 by GIA Publications, Inc., 7404 S. Mason Ave., Chicago, IL 60638 (www.giamusic.com; 800.442.1358). All rights reserved. Used by permission.

Frederick Buechner, *The Faces of Jesus* (Croton-on-Hudson, NY: Riverwood Publishers Limited, and New York: Simon and Schuster, 1974), 172

Bernard of Clairvaux, *O Sacred Head*, *Now Wounded*, 12th century, English tr. James W. Alexander, 1830. Public domain.

Thomas à Kempis, *O Love, How Deep, How Broad, How High*, 15th century, tr. Benjamin Webb, 1854. Public domain.

Trisagion, ancient hymn. Public domain.

Solemn Reproaches of the Cross, 9th-11th centuries. Public domain.

Jane Dillenberger, *Secular Art with Sacred Themes* (Nashville: Abingdon Press, 1969), 44-47

Charles Wesley, *And Can It Be*, 1738. Public domain.

Calvin Seerveld, *Bearing Fresh Olive Leaves: Alternative Steps in Understanding Art* (Carlisle, UK: Piquant, and Toronto: Tuppence Press, 2000), 84-85

T. S. Eliot, excerpt, "The Family Reunion," from *The Complete Poems and Plays 1909-1950* (New York: Harcourt, Brace & World, 1962), 291

Meekness and Majesty / This Is Your God. Graham Kendrick. © 1986 Thankyou Music (admin. by EMI Christian Music Publishing c/o: Music Services). All Rights Reserved. Used By Permission.

Alexander Means, *What Wondrous Love Is This*, 1835. Public domain.

Anneke Kaai and Eugene H. Peterson, *In a Word: See What You Believe* (Brewster, MA: Paraclete Press, and Carlisle, UK: Piquant, 2003), 58

This Is the Mind-Set of One Who Has Come. Words: Shirley Erena Murray. © 1996 Hope Publishing Company, Carol Stream, IL 60188. All rights reserved. Used by permission.

Down from the Height of His Glory He Came. Words: Michael A. Perry. © 1986 The Jubilate Group (admin. Hope Publishing Company, Carol Stream, IL 60188). All rights reserved. Used by permission.

Name of All Majesty. Words: Timothy Dudley-Smith. © 1984 Hope Publishing Company, Carol Stream, IL 60188. All rights reserved. Used by permission.

F. Bland Tucker, *All Praise to Christ*, 1938. © The Church Pension Group

You, Lord, Are Both Lamb and Shepherd / Christus Paradox. Sylvia G. Dunstan. Copyright © 1991 by GIA Publications, Inc., 7404 S. Mason Ave., Chicago, IL 60638 (www.giamusic.com; 800.442.1358). All rights reserved. Used by permission.

2:12-13 God at Work

section intro. text

Dag Hammarskjöld, *Markings*, tr. Leif Sjöberg and W. H. Auden (New York: Alfred A. Knopf, Inc., 1964), 205

William Barclay, *The Gospel of Matthew*, vol. 1, The Daily Study Bible Series, 2nd ed. (Philadelphia: Westminster Press, 1958), 119

C. S. Lewis, *The Weight of Glory and Other Addresses*, ed. Walter Hooper (New York: Simon and Schuster, Inc., 1949), 34

Earl F. Palmer, *Integrity: A Commentary on the Book of Philippians* (Vancouver, CA: Regent College Publishing, 2000; orig. ed. InterVarsity Press, 1992, as *Integrity in a World of Pretense: Insights from the Book of Philippians*), 105-6

2:12b-13

Karl Barth, *The Epistle to the Philippians*, tr. James W. Leitch, 40th Anniversary Edition (Louisville and London: Westminster John Knox Press, 2002), 72

Jane Dillenberger, *Image and Spirit in Sacred and Secular Art*, ed. Diane Apostolos-Cappadona (New York: Crossroad Publishing Company, 1990), 34

The Belgic Confession, excerpt from Article 24, from *The Psalter Hymnal* (Grand Rapids, MI: CRC Publications, 1987), 840

The Life Laid Down Is Taken Up Again. Words: Carl P. Daw, Jr. © 2001, 2006 Hope Publishing Company, Carol Stream, IL 60188. All rights reserved. Used by permission.

Michael Yaconelli, www.youthspecialties.com/yaconelli/words/wordsfrommike.php

Where the Love of God Is Guiding. Words: Shirley Erena Murray. © 1999 Hope Publishing Company, Carol Stream, IL 60188. All rights reserved. Used by permission.

With Trembling Bliss of Eager Hearts. Text: David A. Robb, 1990. Text © 2000 Selah Publishing Co., Inc. www.selahpub.com. All rights reserved. Used by permission.

Abraham Joshua Heschel, *I Asked for Wonder: A Spiritual Anthology*, ed. Samuel H. Dresner (New York: Crossroad Publishing Company, 1985), 2

Eugene H. Peterson, *Christ Plays in Ten Thousand Places: A Conversation in Spiritual Theology* (Grand Rapids, MI, and Cambridge, UK: Wm. B. Eerdmans Publishing Company, 2005), 43-44

2:14-18 Life Revealed

2:14

William H. M. H. Aitken, *The Prayer at Eventide* (London: J. F. Shaw & Co., 1878)

Paul Detterman, 2007. Public domain.

2:15

Kathleen Powers Erickson, *At Eternity's Gate: The Spiritual Vision of Vincent van Gogh* (Grand Rapids, MI, and Cambridge, UK: Wm. B. Eerdmans Publishing Company, 1998), 65, 82, 165

Taizé Community, *Prayer for Each Day* (Chicago: GIA; London: Cassell, 1998), 73. Copyright © 1997, 1998, Ateliers et Presses de Taizé, Taizé Community, France. GIA Publications, Inc., exclusive North American agent, 7404 S. Mason Ave., Chicago, IL 60638 (www.giamusic.com; 800.442.1358). All rights reserved. Used by permission.

Rory Cooney, Do Not Fear to Hope © 1986, 2000, spiritandsong.com®, 5536 NE Hassalo, Portland OR 97213. All rights reserved. Used with permission.

2:16

Beyond the Beauty and the Awe. Words: Carl P. Daw, Jr. © 1994 Hope Publishing Company, Carol Stream, IL 60188. All rights reserved. Used by permission.

Church in Wales, from *Prayers Encircling the World: An International Anthology of 300 Contemporary Prayers* (Great Britain: SPCK, 1998; Louisville: Westminster John Knox Press, 1999), 246 #299. Reprinted by permission of the Anglican Consultative Council.

2:19-30 Paul's Humanity

section intro. text

Karl Barth, *The Epistle to the Philippians*, tr. James W. Leitch, 40th Anniversary Edition (Louisville and London: Westminster John Knox Press, 2002), 9

2:19

Sgt. Jessica Billstrom, "Soldiers' letters home capture war's untold stories," *The Milwaukee Journal Sentinel*, Aug. 29, 2004.

2:22

Jane L. Borthwick, *Come, Labor On*, 1859, rev. 1863. Public domain.

2:29-30

Henri J. M. Nouwen, *Behold the Beauty of the Lord: Praying with Icons* (Notre Dame, IN: Ave Maria Press, 1987), 23

Richard Baxter, *The Practical Works of the Rev. Richard Baxter: With a Life of the Author, and a Critical Examination of His Writings, by the Rev. William Orme, in Twenty-Three Volumes*, vol. IV (London: James Duncan, 1830), 340

3:1-11 Affirming Priorities

section intro. text

Karl Barth, *The Epistle to the Philippians*, tr. James W. Leitch,

40th Anniversary Edition (Louisville and London: Westminster John Knox Press, 2002), 103

Rebecca Manley Pippert, *Hope Has Its Reasons: The Search to Satisfy Our Deepest Longings*, rev. ed. (Downers Grove, IL: InterVarsity Press, 2001), 179

3:1

The Psalter: A Faithful and Inclusive Rendering from the Hebrew into Contemporary English Poetry, Intended Primarily for Communal Song and Recitation, ed. Gabe Huck (Chicago: Liturgy Training Publications, 1995)

3:2-3

Calvin Seerveld, *Voicing God's Psalms* (Grand Rapids, MI, and Cambridge, UK: Wm. B. Eerdmans Publishing Company, 2005), 37. © 2005 Calvin Seerveld. Reprinted by permission of the publisher. All rights reserved.

Brother Roger, *Life from Within: Prayers by Brother Roger of Taizé* (London: Geoffrey Chapman Mowbray; Louisville: Westminster/John Knox Press, 1990), 22. Copyright © 1990, Ateliers et Presses de Taizé, Taizé Community, France. GIA Publications, Inc., exclusive North American agent, 7404 S. Mason Ave., Chicago, IL 60638 (*www.giamusic.com*; 800.442.1358). All rights reserved. Used by permission.

Calvin Seerveld, excerpt, *A Congregational Lament / Why, Lord, Must Evil Seem to Get Its Way?*, 1986, alt. © Calvin Seerveld. Used by permission.

Jessie Schut, "Lord, you said . . . ," *Reformed Worship* 64 (June 2002): 24. Copyright © 2002 Faith Alive Christian Resources. Used by permission.

3:3-6

Jeffrey Carlson, "Dear God, silence all voices . . . ," *Reformed Worship* 19 (March 1991): 31, alt. Copyright © 1991 Faith Alive Christian Resources. Used by permission.

PC(USA), excerpt, *A Brief Statement of Faith*, www.pcusa.org/101/101-faith.htm

Polycarp, *The Letter of Saint Polycarp, Bishop of Smyrna, to the Philippians*, from *The Library of Christian Classics*, vol. I: *Early Christian Fathers*, ed. Cyril C. Richardson

(Philadelphia: Westminster Press, and London: S.C.M. Press, Ltd., 1953), 131

Unknown, *Be Thou My Vision*, 8th century (tr. Mary E. Byrne, 1905; vers. Eleanor Hull, 1912). Public domain.

3:7-9

The Psalter: A Faithful and Inclusive Rendering from the Hebrew into Contemporary English Poetry, Intended Primarily for Communal Song and Recitation, ed. Gabe Huck (Chicago: Liturgy Training Publications, 1995)

Michael Yaconelli, *Messy Spirituality: God's Annoying Love for Imperfect People* (Grand Rapids, MI: Zondervan, 2002), 93

Amazing Love / My Lord, What Love Is This. Graham Kendrick. © 1989 Make Way Music (admin. by Music Services in the Western Hemisphere). All rights reserved. ASCAP

Karl Barth, *The Epistle to the Philippians*, tr. James W. Leitch, 40th Anniversary Edition (Louisville and London: Westminster John Knox Press, 2002), 98

3:10

Charles William Everest, *Take Up Your Cross, the Savior Said*, 1833. Public domain.

Robin M. Jensen, *The Substance of Things Seen: Art, Faith, and the Christian Community* (Grand Rapids, MI, and Cambridge, UK: Wm. B. Eerdmans Publishing Company, 2004), 43-44

Perpetual God, Unchanging Source. James Hart Brumm, 1988. © 2010 Wayne Leupold Editions, Inc. Used by permission. www.wayneleupold.com

Knowing You / All I Once Held Dear. Graham Kendrick. © 1994 Make Way Music (admin. by Music Services in the Western Hemisphere). All rights reserved. ASCAP

3:11

Scott E. Hoezee, "The Movement of Philippians 3," 2005

Apostles' Creed, c. A.D 700. Public domain.

Wassily Kandinsky, *Concerning the Spiritual in Art*, tr. M. T. H. Sadler (New York: Dover Publications, Inc., 1977), 38

George Herbert, "Easter," 1633, from *The Works of George Herbert*, ed. F. E. Hutchinson (London: Oxford at the Clarendon Press, 1941), 41-42

In the Winter of Our Spirits. John Core, 2005. © 2006 Wayne Leupold Editions, Inc. Used by permission. www.wayneleupold.com

3:12-14 Unpacking the Mystery

3:12

Eric Milner-White and George Wallace Briggs, comp., *Daily Prayer* (London: Oxford University Press, 1941), 14, alt., as found in *Book of Common Worship* (Louisville: Westminster/John Knox Press, 1993), 501 #6 [446]. Used by permission.

Unknown, *Guide My Feet* (African American spiritual). Public domain.

3:13-14

M. J. Anderson, sculptor, 2005

Michael Morgan, *The Psalter for Christian Worship* (Witherspoon Press, Louisville, KY; Office of Theology and Worship, Louisville, KY; Columbia Theological Seminary, Decatur, GA, 1999), 151. © 1999 Michael Morgan. Used by permission.

Church in Uganda, from *Prayers Encircling the World: An International Anthology of 300 Contemporary Prayers* (Great Britain: SPCK, 1998; Louisville: Westminster John Knox Press, 1999), 102 #114. Reprinted by permission of the Anglican Consultative Council.

Ahead of Us, A Race to Run. Martin E. Leckebusch. © 2000. Reproduced by permission of Kevin Mayhew Ltd. (www.kevinmayhew.com). Licence nr. 906091/1.

E. Lee Phillips, *Breaking Silence Before the Lord: Worship Prayers* (Grand Rapids, MI: Baker Books, 1986), 69 #8. © 1986 Baker Books, a division of Baker Publishing Group.

Isaac Watts, *O God, Our Help in Ages Past*, 1719. Public domain.

3:15-21 Eager Hope

section intro. text

Cornelius Plantinga, Jr., *Beyond Doubt: Faith-Building Devotions on Questions Christians Ask* (Grand Rapids, MI, and Cambridge, UK: Wm. B. Eerdmans Publishing Company, 2002), 201

Rebecca Manley Pippert, *Hope Has Its Reasons: The Search to Satisfy Our Deepest Longings*, rev. ed. (Downers Grove, IL: InterVarsity Press, 2001), 13, 178, 194

Stuart Briscoe, *Philippians: Happiness Beyond Our Happenings*, rev. ed. (Wheaton, IL: Harold Shaw Publishers, 1993), 113, 111

P. T. Forsyth, in M. Craig Barnes, *Extravagant Mercy: Reflections on Ordinary Things* (Ann Arbor: Servant Publications, 2003), 19

M. Craig Barnes, *Extravagant Mercy: Reflections on Ordinary Things* (Ann Arbor: Servant Publications, 2003), 19

3:17-19

Here I Am / Kata ku nani mo. Yukiko Ishiyama, Japan; tr. Yasuhiko Yokosaka. Copyright © 1990, 2000, Christian Conference of Asia, admin. GIA Publications, Inc., 7404 S. Mason Ave., Chicago, IL 60638 (www.giamusic.com; 800.442.1358). All rights reserved. Used by permission.

Free to Serve / When We Walk Alone and Work for Self. Words & Music: Tom Colvin. © 1969 Hope Publishing Company, Carol Stream, IL 60188. All rights reserved. Used by permission.

Far from Home We Run Rebellious. Herman G. Stuempfle, Jr. Copyright © 1993 by GIA Publications, Inc., 7404 S. Mason Ave., Chicago, IL 60638 (www.giamusic.com; 800.442.1358). All rights reserved. Used by permission.

3:20-21

Robert Lowry, *My Life Flows On in Endless Song / How Can I Keep from Singing?*, 1869. Public domain.

Nicolaus L. von Zinzendorf, *Jesus, Still Lead On*, 1721; tr. Jane L. Borthwick, 1846. Public domain.

Polycarp, *The Letter of Saint Polycarp, Bishop of Smyrna, to the Philippians*, from *The Library of Christian Classics*, vol. I: *Early Christian Fathers*, ed. Cyril C. Richardson (Philadelphia: Westminster Press, and London: S.C.M. Press, Ltd., 1953), 133

4:1-7 In the Lord

section intro. text

Moisés Silva, *Philippians*, 2nd ed. (Baker Exegetical Commentary on the New Testament), ed. Robert Yarbrough and Robert H. Stein (Grand Rapids, MI: Baker Academic, 2005), 193

Dietrich Bonhoeffer, *The Cost of Discipleship*, 2nd ed., tr. R. H. Fuller, rev. Irmgard Booth (New York: Macmillan Company, 1959), 85

Earl F. Palmer, *Integrity: A Commentary on the Book of Philippians* (Vancouver, CA: Regent College Publishing, 2000; orig. ed. InterVarsity Press, 1992, as *Integrity in a World of Pretense: Insights from the Book of Philippians*), 152

Sarah Cunningham, *Dear Church: Letters from a Disillusioned Generation* (Grand Rapids, MI: Zondervan, 2006), 165-67

In the Lord I'll Be Ever Thankful. Taizé Community. Copyright © 1991, Les Presses de Taizé, Taizé Community, France. GIA Publications, Inc., exclusive North American agent, 7404 S. Mason Ave., Chicago, IL 60638 (www.giamusic.com; 800.442.1358). All rights reserved. Used by permission.

4:1

Irenaeus of Sirmium, from *The Communion of Saints: Prayers of the Famous*, ed. Horton Davies (Grand Rapids, MI: Wm. B. Eerdmans Publishing Company, 1990), 6

Polycarp, *The Letter of Saint Polycarp, Bishop of Smyrna, to the Philippians*, from *The Library of Christian Classics*, vol. I: *Early Christian Fathers*, ed. Cyril C. Richardson (Philadelphia: Westminster Press, and London: S.C.M. Press, Ltd., 1953), 134-35

Edward Mote, *My Hope Is Built on Nothing Less / The Solid Rock*, c.1834. Public domain.

Gerhard Tersteegen, from *The Westminster Collection of Christian Prayers*, comp. Dorothy M. Stewart (Louisville and London: Westminster John Knox, 2002), 52 #26.3

4:2-3

Thomas G. Long, sermon excerpt, January 27, 2005

Polycarp, *The Letter of Saint Polycarp, Bishop of Smyrna, to the Philippians*, from *The Library of Christian Classics*, vol. I: *Early Christian Fathers*, ed. Cyril C. Richardson (Philadelphia: Westminster Press, and London: S.C.M. Press, Ltd., 1953), 134

Hope Publishing Company, Carol Stream, IL 60188). All rights reserved. Used by permission.

Nathan D. Mitchell, "Being Beautiful, Being Just," essay from *Toward Ritual Transformation: Remembering Robert W. Hovda* (Collegeville, MN: Liturgical Press, 2003), 72-73

Hans K. Roethel, *Kandinsky* (New York: Hudson Hills Press, 1979), 76

Samuel Stennett, *I Am Bound for the Promised Land / On Jordan's Stormy Banks I Stand*, 1787. Public domain.

Bennett P. Samuel, *what about justice*, 2008. Based on Philippians 4:8-9 (NIV). Used by permission.

4:10-20 Contentment

section intro. text

Gordon D. Fee, *Paul's Letter to the Philippians*, The New International Commentary on the New Testament, ed. Gordon D. Fee (Grand Rapids, MI: Wm. B. Eerdmans Publishing Company, 1995), 426

Bill Hybels, *Run the Race: Philippians* (Grand Rapids, MI: Zondervan, 1999), 58

Richard J. Foster, *Money, Sex & Power: The Challenge of the Disciplined Life* (San Francisco: Harper and Row, Publishers, 1985), 33

Frank Thielman, *Philippians*, The NIV Application Commentary (Grand Rapids, MI: Zondervan Publishing House, 1995), 243

Jacques Ellul, *Money and Power*, tr. LaVonne Neff (Downers Grove, IL: InterVarsity Press, 1984), 110

4:10-13

Kathleen Powers Erickson, *At Eternity's Gate: The Spiritual Vision of Vincent van Gogh* (Grand Rapids, MI, and Cambridge, UK: Wm. B. Eerdmans Publishing Company, 1998), 86, 88-89

Dietrich Bonhoeffer, from "A Wedding Sermon from a Prison Cell, May 1943," in *Letters and Papers from Prison*, ed. Eberhard Bethge, tr. Reginald H. Fuller (London: SCM Press, Ltd., 1956), 31-32

Ignatius, *The Letters of Ignatius*, Bishop of Antioch: To the Ephesians, from *The Library of Christian Classics*, vol. I: *Early Christian Fathers*, ed. Cyril C. Richardson (Philadelphia: Westminster Press, and London: S.C.M. Press, Ltd., 1953), 93

Martha Moore-Keish, from *A More Profound Alleluia: Theology and Worship in Harmony*, ed. Leanne Van Dyk (Grand Rapids, MI, and Cambridge, UK: Wm. B. Eerdmans Publishing Company, 2005), 117-18

Before You, Lord, Who Can Pretend? (Psalm 131). Words: Carl P. Daw, Jr. © 2001 Hope Publishing Company, Carol Stream, IL 60188. All rights reserved. Used by permission.

John Calvin, *Institutes of the Christian Religion*, ed. John T. McNeill, tr. Ford Lewis Battles (Philadelphia: Westminster Press, 1960), 4.17.1, 1360-61

W. H. Auden, excerpt, "Compline," from "Horae Canonicae," *Selected Poetry of W. H. Auden* (New York: Modern Library, 1959), 172

Anonymous, *I Sought the Lord, and Afterward I Knew*, 1878. Public domain.

4:18

Bring We the Frankincense of Our Love. H. Kenn Carmichael. © 1978 H. Kenn Carmichael. All rights reserved. Used by permission of H. Kenn Carmichael estate.

John Calvin, *La forme des prieres, Joannis Calvini opera selecta*, ed. P. Barth et al., 5 vols. (Munich: Chr. Kaiser, 1926-62), vol. 2 (1952), 41-42; tr. from Elsie A. McKee, *John Calvin on the Diaconate and Liturgical Almsgiving* (Geneva: Librarie Droz, 1984), 50

God, Whose Giving Knows No Ending. Words: Robert L. Edwards. © 1961, ren. 1989 The Hymn Society (admin. Hope Publishing Company, Carol Stream, IL 60188). All rights reserved. Used by permission.

4:19-20

Luke Connaughton, Reap Me the Earth as a Harvest for God, alt. © McCrimmon Publishing, Great Wakering, SS3 0EQ Essex, England

The Holy Gifts of God. Text: Rae E. Whitney, 1978, 1985. Text © 1995 Selah Publishing Co., Inc. www.selahpub.com. All rights reserved. Used by permission.

For Your Generous Providing. Leith Fisher. © 1998 Panel on Worship. Used by permission.

The Psalter: A Faithful and Inclusive Rendering from the Hebrew into Contemporary English Poetry, Intended Primarily for Communal Song and Recitation, ed. Gabe Huck (Chicago: Liturgy Training Publications, 1995)

Lutheran Book of Worship: Minister's Desk Edition, alt. Copyright © 1978, by permission of Augsburg Fortress.

4:21-23 Grace and Peace

section intro. text

John S. B. Monsell, *On Our Way Rejoicing*, 1863, rev. 1873. Public domain.

4:21-23

Cyril of Jerusalem, from *Catechetical Lecture 23 (On the Mysteries. V.)*, *On the Sacred Liturgy and Communion*, *1 Pet. ii:3*, from *A Select Library of the Nicene and Post-Nicene Fathers of the Christian Church* (Second Series), vol. VII: *Cyril of Jerusalem, Gregory Nazianzan*, ed. Philip Schaff and Henry Wace (Edinburgh: T & T Clark; Grand Rapids: Wm. B. Eerdmans Publishing Company, 1974), 153

attr. John Fawcett, *Lord, Dismiss Us with Your Blessing*, 1773. Public domain.

Prayers for Contemporary Worship (Edinburgh: Saint Andrew Press, 1977), 89. © 1977 Church of Scotland Committee on Public Worship and Aids to Devotion. Used by permission.

Image Sources

(in order of appearance)

Cover

Gustav Klimt, *Pear Tree*, 1903
Klimt, Gustav (1862-1918). Pear Tree. 1903 (later reworked). Oil on canvas, 101 x 101 cm (39 3/4 x 39 3/4 in.). Gift of Otto Kallir, BR66.4. Photo: Katya Kallsen. Busch-Reisinger Museum, Harvard Art Museum, Cambridge, Massachusetts, U.S.A. © Harvard Art Museum / Art Resource, NY.

Introduction

Vincent van Gogh, *Olive Trees, Pink Sky*, 1889
Gogh, Vincent van (1853-1890). Olive Trees, Pink Sky. 1889. Van Gogh Museum, Amsterdam, The Netherlands. Photo Credit: Art Resource, NY.

Cornelis Monsma, *Where We Meet (Psalm 85:10-11)*, 1999
Oil on canvas, 80 x 100 cm (32 x 40 in.). © 1999 Cornelis Monsma. Used by permission. www.monsmart.com

Timothy R. Botts, *Philippians 4:8*, 2000
Calligraphy. *The Holy Bible, Botts Illustrated Edition*, Tyndale, 2000. Calligraphy by Timothy R. Botts. Used by permission.

View of Philippi's archaeological site from the acropolis. The forum is in the foreground; the market and "Basilica B" are in the background. Photography taken 12/11/2000 by Marsyas. File licensed under the Creative Commons Attribution ShareAlike 3.0 License, http://creativecommons.org/licenses/by-sa/3.0

Johannes Vermeer, *Woman Reading a Letter*, c. 1662-63
Oil on canvas, 46.5 x 39 cm. © Rijksmuseum Amsterdam, The Netherlands. Photoarchive Rijksmuseum Amsterdam.

Martin Bulinya, *Untitled*
Acrylic and ink on paper, 8 1/2 x 12 1/4 in. From the collection of Elizabeth Steele Halstead.

Don Prys, *Song of the Prairie*, 2004
Mixed media. © 2004 Don Prys. Used by permission. From the collection of Roberta Aldaag-Lentz.

1:1-2 Grace and Peace

1:1a

Randy Beumer, *Written in Shackles*, 2006
Pencil on paper. © 2006 Randy Beumer. Used by permission. From the collection of the Calvin Institute of Christian Worship.

1:1b

Communion of Saints, Cathedral of Our Lady of the Angels, Los Angeles, California, 2001-02
Cotton and viscose tapestries designed by John R. Nava. Woven by Flanders Tapestries. www.olacathedral.org/cathedral/art/tapestries.html

Scott Mutter, *Untitled (Church Aisle)*, 1986
Gelatine-silver print photomontage. © 1986 Scott Mutter. All Rights Reserved. Used by permission of Estate of Scott Mutter.

1:2

Makoto Fujimura, *Grace Foretold*, 1998
102 x 80 in., Mineral Pigments, Gold on Kumohada. © Makoto Fujimura, 1998.

Anneke Kaai, *Peace* 2003, acrylic on plexiglas. From Anneke Kaai & Eugene Peterson, *In a Word* (2003), 51. Used with permission. www.piquanteditions.com

1:3-11 Confident Prayer

1:3-5

Bernadette Lopez, *Je crois à la communion des saints*, 2003
Acrylic. © 2003 Bernadette Lopez. Used by permission. www.evangile-et-peinture.org

Don Prys, *Song of the Prairie*, 2004
Mixed media. © 2004 Don Prys. Used by permission. From the collection of Roberta Aldaag-Lentz.

1:6

Timothy R. Botts, *Philippians 1:6*, 2000
Calligraphy. *The Holy Bible, Botts Illustrated Edition*, Tyndale, 2000. Calligraphy by Timothy R. Botts. Used by permission.

1:7-8

Rembrandt Harmensz. van Rijn, *Saint Paul in Prison*, 1627
Rembrandt (Rembrandt Harmensz. van Rijn): Paulus im Gefängnis / St. Paul in Prison, 1627, Öl auf Eichenholz (Oil on Oak), 72.8 cm x 60.3 cm (Inv. 0746). © Staatsgalerie Stuttgart. Foto: Staatsgalerie Stuttgart.

Lisa Ellis, *Miriam's Dance*, 2006
Fiber art, 36 1/2 x 33 in. Photograph printed courtesy of the artist. © 2006 Lisa Ellis. www.ellisquilts.com

1:9-10a

Jan L. Richardson, *Wisdom's Path*, 1998
Mixed media. © 1998 Jan L. Richardson. Used by permission. www.janrichardson.com

1:10b-11

Gustav Klimt, *Pear Tree*, 1903
Klimt, Gustav (1862-1918) Pear Tree. 1903 (later reworked). Oil on canvas, 101 x 101 cm (39 3/4 x 39 3/4 in.). Gift of Otto Kallir, BR66.4. Photo: Katya Kallsen. Busch-Reisinger Museum, Harvard Art Museum, Cambridge, Massachusetts, U.S.A. © Harvard Art Museum / Art Resource, NY.

Eric Nykamp, *Grow Where You Are Planted*, 2002
Acrylic on canvas. © 2002 Eric Nykamp. Used by permission. From the collection of Jeffery Jackson.

1:11

John August Swanson, *Psalm 85*, 2003
Psalm 85 © 2003 by John August Swanson. Serigraph 24 x 28 3/4 in. www.JohnAugustSwanson.com Los Angeles artist John August Swanson is noted for his finely detailed, brilliantly colored paintings and original prints. His works are found in the Smithsonian Institution's National Museum of American History, London's Tate Gallery, the Vatican Museum's Collection of Modern Religious Art, and the Bibliothèque Nationale, Paris. Full-color posters and cards of Mr. Swanson's work are available from the National Association for Hispanic Elderly.

1:12-21 Divine Purpose

1:12-14

Paul Klee, *Untitled (Trapped) / Captive (Figure of this world/next world)*, c.1940
Oil, drawing with colored paste on burlap with a paste ground mounted on burlap, 55.20 x 50.10 cm. Fondation Beyeler, Riehen / Basel © 2009 Artists Rights Society (ARS), New York / VG Bild-Kunst, Bonn.

Rachel Durfee, *For Those in Captivity*, 2002
Rachel Durfee, "For Those in Captivity", © 2002, woodcut with hand coloring, 23 1/2 x 20 1/2 in., All Rights Reserved, Used by Permission of the Artist.

Steve Prince, *9 Little Indians: Letter to the Public Schools*, 2004
Linoleum cut. © 2009 Steve Prince | Eyekons. www.eyekons.com

1:15-18a

Bryan Hiott, *Divine Lite*, 1999
Digital photograph, 11 x 14 in. © 2001 The Episcopal Church and Visual Arts. www.ecva.org/exhibition/light/pages/hiott.html

1:18b-19

Ken Glaser, *Hands of Inmate on Cell Bars*
Corbis Premium RF / Alamy

James Fissel, *Bethlehem's Star*, 2005
Mixed media. © 2009 James Fissel | Eyekons. www.eyekons.com

1:20

Tim Ladwig, *Our Father in Heaven*, from *The Lord's Prayer*, 2000
Watercolor. Tim Ladwig, *Our Father in Heaven*, from *The Lord's Prayer* © 2000 Wm. B. Eerdmans Publishing Company, Grand Rapids, MI. Reprinted by permission of the publisher; all rights reserved.

Bagong Kussudiardja, *The Ascension*, 1984
Oil on canvas. From Maseo Takenaka and Ron O'Grady, *The Bible Through Asian Eyes* (Auckland, NZ: Pace Publishing; Kyoto, Japan: in association with the Asian Christian Art Association, 1991), 165. Copyright © 1991 Asian Christian Art Association.

1:22-30 Standing Firm

Jean-François Millet, *The Angelus*, 1857
Millet, Jean-François. The Angelus, 1857. Oil on canvas, 55.5 x 66 cm. Musée d'Orsay, Paris, France. Photo Credit: Erich Lessing / Art Resource, NY.

Edicio de la Torre, *Kalayaan (Freedom)*, 1979
Oil on canvas. From Masao Takenaka and Ron O'Grady, *The Bible Through Asian Eyes* (Auckland, NZ: Pace Publishing; Kyoto, Japan: in association with the Asian Christian Art Association, 1991), 177. Copyright © 1991 Asian Christian Art Association.

Jan L. Richardson, *The Wise Ones*, 1997
Mixed media. © 1997 Jan L. Richardson. Used by permission. www.janrichardson.com

Magrit Prigge, *Fiery Furnace*, 2002
© Magrit Prigge, 'Fiery Furnace', Watercolor, 2002. www.AllTribesArts.com

2:1-4 Finding One Mind

Joseph O'Connell, *Community*, 1985
Limestone. From Colman O'Connell, O.S.B., ed., *Divine Favor: The Art of Joseph O'Connell* (Liturgical Press, 1999), 53. © 1999 by The Order of Saint Benedict Inc., Collegeville, MN.

Leonard Freed, *Return of Martin Luther King Jr., after receiving Nobel Peace Prize*, Baltimore, 1963 (photo detail)
From *Leonard Freed: Photographs 1954-1990* (W. W.

Norton, 1991), 41. Copyright 1991 by Les Editions Nathan, Paris. First American edition, 1992. Originally published in France under the title, *Photographies 1954-1990*, par Leonard Freed. W. W. Norton & Co., Inc. and Ltd.

2:2a

John August Swanson, *Celebration*, 1997
Celebration © 1997 by John August Swanson. Serigraph 22 1/2 x 30 1/2 in. www.JohnAugustSwanson.com Los Angeles artist John August Swanson is noted for his finely detailed, brilliantly colored paintings and original prints. His works are found in the Smithsonian Institution's National Museum of American History, London's Tate Gallery, the Vatican Museum's Collection of Modern Religious Art, and the Bibliothèque Nationale, Paris. Full-color posters and cards of Mr. Swanson's work are available from the National Association for Hispanic Elderly.

Elizabeth Steele Halstead, *The Heavens and the Earth*, 1985
Woodcut, 19 x 15 in. © 1985 Elizabeth Steele Halstead. Used by permission.

Emil Nolde, *Wildtanzende Kinder (Wildly Dancing Children)*, 1909
Wildtanzende Kinder (Wildly Dancing Children), 1909, oil on canvas, 73 x 88 cm. Kiel, Kunsthalle zu Kiel (Wvz Urban 315). © Nolde Stiftung Seebüll.

2:2b

Paul Stoub, *Children of the Light*, 1973
Woodcut. © 1973 by Paul Stoub. Used by permission.

Saint Hildegard von Bingen (1098-1179), *"All creation praises the Lord," the nine choirs of the angels*, from *Liber Scivias (Know the ways of the Lord)*
Saint Hildegard of Bingen (1098-1179). "All creation praises the Lord," the nine choirs of the angels, from "Liber Scivias" (Know the ways of the Lord) by Hildegard von Bingen. From a facsimile. Photo Credit: Erich Lessing / Art Resource, NY.

2:3-4

Dinah Roe Kendall, *Jesus Washing the Disciples' Feet*, 1996
Dinah Roe Kendall, Jesus Washing the Disciples' Feet

(1996), acrylic on canvas. From Dinah Roe Kendall & Eugene Peterson, *Allegories of Heaven* (2003), 69. Used with permission. www.piquanteditions.com

2:5-11 Imitating Christ

2:5

Rick Beerhorst, *The Imitation of Christ*, 2005
  Oil on board. © 2009 Rick Beerhorst | Eyekons. www.eyekons.com

Laurel Lozzi, *Mary and Martha*, 2006
  Photo collage. © 2006 Laurel Lozzi. Used by permission.

2:6-8

Sandra Bowden, *In the Beginning Was the Word*, 1982
  Collagraph and embossing, 30 x 18 in. © 1982 Sandra Bowden. Used by permission.

Anonymous, *Christ with the Crown of Thorns*, 20th century
  Wood sculpture. Reproduced from *The Faces of Jesus* by Frederick Buechner with photographs by Lee Boltin, published by Harper & Row, © 1989, with permission from Stearn Publishers Ltd.

Bruce Herman, *The Crowning*, 1991
  Pastel and mixed media on paper, 38 x 45 in. The Crowning (from the series Golgotha) © Bruce Herman, 1991. Collection of Ed and Margaret Killeen. Bruce Herman, Lothlórien Distinguished Chair in the Fine Arts, Gallery Director, Gordon College. http://bruceherman.com

Henri Matisse, *Icarus*, plate VIII from the illustrated book "Jazz," 1947
  Matisse, Henri (1869-1954). Icarus, plate VIII from the illustrated book "Jazz." Stencil print, published by Teriade 1947, in an edition of 270 copies. Twenty pochoir plates, each double sheet 42.2 x 65.1 cm. © 2009 Succession H. Matisse / Artists Rights Society (ARS), New York. Photo: Archives Henri Matisse.

Marc Chagall, *White Crucifixion*, 1938
  Marc Chagall, French, born Vitebsk, Russia (present-day Belarus), 1887-1985, White Crucifixion, 1938, Oil on canvas, 154.3 x 139.7 cm, Gift of Alfred S. Alschuler, 1946.925, The Art Institute of Chicago. Photography

© The Art Institute of Chicago. © 2009 Artists Rights Society (ARS), New York / ADAGP, Paris.

Mathias Gruenewald, *Crucifixion*. A panel from the Isenheim Altar, c.1515
  Gruenewald, Mathias (1455-1528). Crucifixion. A panel from the Isenheim Altar. Limewood (around 1515). 260 x 650 cm. Musée d'Unterlinden, Colmar, France. Photo Credit: Erich Lessing / Art Resource, NY.

Pablo Picasso, *The Crucifixion*, 1930
  Picasso, Pablo (1881-1973). The Crucifixion, 1930. Oil on plywood. 51.5 x 66.5 cm. MP 122. Photo: R. G. Ojeda. Musée Picasso, Paris, France. © 2009 Estate of Pablo Picasso / Artists Rights Society (ARS), New York. Photo Credit: Réunion des Musées Nationaux / Art Resource, NY.

Kevin Rolly, *Forsaken (The Crucifixion)*, 2005
  Mixed media oilgraph on canvas. © 2005 Kevin Rolly. Used by permission.

Michael Angel, *Waterfall II (Psalm 42:7)*, 2007
  Acrylic. © 2007 by Michael Angel. Used by permission. www.MichaelAngelArt.com

Daniel Bonnell, *Upside Down Sunset*
  © Daniel Bonnell. All rights reserved. Used by permission. www.BonnellArt.com

Giotto di Bondone (1266-1336), *Pieta (Lamentation)*, detail
  Giotto di Bondone (1266-1336). Pieta (Lamentation). Scrovegni Chapel, Padua, Italy. Photo Credit: Alinari / Art Resource, NY.

Hans Holbein the Younger, *Dead Christ*, 1521
  Holbein, Hans the Younger (1497-1543). Dead Christ. 1521. Kunstmuseum, Basel, Switzerland. Photo Credit: Erich Lessing / Art Resource, NY.

Makoto Fujimura, *Gravity and Grace*, 2002
  66 x 89 in., Cinnabar, Vermillion on Kumohada. © Makoto Fujimura, 2002.

Anneke Kaai, *Death*, 2001
  Anneke Kaai, Death (2001). Acrylic and mixed media on plexiglas. From Anneke Kaai & Eugene Peterson, *In a Word* (2003), 39. Used with permission. www.piquanteditions.com

2:9

Yuyu Yang, *The Cross*, 1964
Copper and oil painting, 116 x 61 x 14 cm. With permission by the Yuyu Yang Education Foundation.

C. Robin Janning, *Some Mercy*, 2007
Acrylics on paper. © 2007 C. Robin Janning. Used by permission.

Baptistry window, Cathedral Church of St. Michael, Coventry, England, 1962
Ian M. Butterfield Alamy

Folio from the Missal of Abbess de Munchensey (Christ in Glory)
Folio uit een missaal van abdis de Munchensey, illumination on parchment. Museum Mayer van den Bergh, Antwerpen © collectiebeleid.

2:10-11

He Qi, *The Risen Lord*, 1998
Color-on-paper painting. © 1998 He Qi. Used by permission. www.heqigallery.com

Laura James, *Psalm 100*, 2004
Acrylics on canvas. © 2004 Laura James. Used by permission. www.laurajamesart.com

Jan van Eyck, *The Adoration of the Lamb*, detail from the Ghent Altarpiece, 1432
Eyck, Jan van (c.1390-1441). The Adoration of the Lamb, detail from the Ghent Altarpiece. 1432. Cathedral of St. Bavo, Ghent, Belgium. Photo Credit: SCALA / Art Resource, NY.

2:12-13 God at Work

2:12b-13

Mary Ann Osborne, *Jonah and the Whale*, 1999
Woodcarving. Photo by John Cross. Used by permission of Mary Ann Osborne, SSND.

Donatello, *Mary Magdalen*, 1453
Donatello (c.1386-1466). Mary Magdalen. 1453. Wood statue. Duomo, Florence, Italy. Photo Credit: Erich Lessing / Art Resource, NY.

Scott Sullivan, *Moses Before the Burning Bush*, 2004
Bas-relief, cold cast. Used with permission from Scott Sullivan, sculptor, at www.scottsullivanart.com.

Ivo Dulcic, *Meal at Emmaus*, 1971
Oil, 80 x 108 cm. Photo: Vatican Museums.

Agnes C. Fisher, *Hannah and Her Children Dance*, 2007
Acrylic on canvas. © 2007 Agnes C. Fisher. Used by permission.

Henry Ossawa Tanner, *The Three Marys*, 1910
Oil on canvas, 40 x 52 in. Fisk University Galleries, Nashville, Tennessee.

Josephine Bloodgood, *Encounter*, 2002
Oil on hardboard. © Josephine Bloodgood. Used by permission.

2:14-18 Life Revealed

2:15

Vincent van Gogh, *The Starry Night*, 1889
Gogh, Vincent van (1853-1890). The Starry Night. 1889. Oil on canvas, 29" x 36 1/4". Acquired through the Lillie P. Bliss Bequest. (472.1941). The Museum of Modern Art, New York, NY, U.S.A. Digital Image © The Museum of Modern Art / Licensed by SCALA / Art Resource, NY.

Alberto Giacometti, *City Square (La Place)*, 1948
Giacometti, Alberto (1901-1966). City Square (La Place). 1948. Bronze, 8 1/2" x 25 3/8" x 17 1/4". (337.1949). The Museum of Modern Art, New York, NY, U.S.A. © 2009 Artists Rights Society (ARS), New York / ADAGP / FAAG, Paris. Digital Image © The Museum of Modern Art / Licensed by SCALA / Art Resource, NY.

Lynn Aldrich, *Island*, 1997
Plastic figures and enamel on half of a globe, 168 x 14 x 9 in. © 1997 Lynn Aldrich. Used by permission.

2:16

Randy Beumer, *How Can I Help?*, 2005
Oil on board. © 2005 Randy Beumer. Used by permission.

Virginio Ciminaghi, *Annunciation*, 1967
Bronze, 94 x 162 x 46 cm. Photo: Vatican Museums.

2:19-30 Paul's Humanity

2:19

Sean Justice, *Soldier Reading Letter from Home*
Corbis Premium RF / Alamy

Johannes Vermeer, *Woman Reading a Letter*,
c.1662-63
Oil on canvas, 46.5 x 39 cm. © Rijksmuseum
Amsterdam, The Netherlands. Photoarchive
Rijksmuseum Amsterdam.

2:22

Margaret Moffett Law, *Laborers*
Watercolor, 18 x 12 in. Reproduced with the permission
of The Charleston Renaissance Gallery, Charleston, South
Carolina.

2:29-30

Andrei Rublev, *Icon of the Old Testament Trinity*, c.1410
Rublev, Andrei (1360-c.1430). Icon of the Old Testament
Trinity. c.1410. Tretyakov Gallery, Moscow, Russia.
Photo Credit: SCALA / Art Resource, NY.

C. Malcolm Powers, *Angelic Greeting*, c. 2000-2001
Cast bronze. © C. Malcolm Powers. Used by permission.

3:1-11 Affirming Priorities

3:1

Doris Klein, *Dance of Delight*, 2000
Doris Klein, Dance of Delight, 2000 © Doris Klein, CSA,
used with permission. Watercolor, approximately 11
x 14 in. Reprints are available from Heartbeats, link
available at www.dorisklein.com.

3:2-3

David Koloane, *Mgodoji II*, 1993
Lithograph. Courtesy the artist and Axis Gallery, NY.

Chris Stoffel Overvoorde, *The Struggle*, 1962
Oil on panel. © 2009 Chris Stoffel Overvoorde |
Eyekons. www.eyekons.com

3:3-6

Karl Schmidt-Rottluff, *Pharisees*, 1912
Schmidt-Rottluff, Karl (1884-1976). Pharisees. 1912. Oil

on canvas, 29 7/8 x 40 1/2″ (75.9 x 102.9 cm). Gertrud
A. Mellon Fund. (160.1955). The Museum of Modern
Art, New York, NY, U.S.A. © 2009 Artists Rights Society
(ARS), New York / VG Bild-Kunst, Bonn. Digital Image
© The Museum of Modern Art / Licensed by SCALA
/ Art Resource, NY.

Fra Angelico, *St. Stephen led to torture
and stoned*, 1448–49
Angelico, Fra (1387-1455). St. Stephen led to torture
and stoned. 1448-1449. Fresco. Cappella Niccolina,
Vatican Palace, Vatican State. Photo Credit: SCALA / Art
Resource, NY.

Norman Rockwell, *The Gossips*, 1948
© 1948 Norman Rockwell Family Entities. Printed by
permission of the Norman Rockwell Family Agency.

3:7-9

John Wells, *Aspiring Forms*, 1950
Oil on board, support: 1067 x 714 mm, frame: 1106 x
758 x 45 mm. © The Estate of John Wells. Photograph
© Tate, London 2009.

3:10

Sandra Bowden, *He Was Wounded for
Our Transgressions*, 1992
Collagraph mixed media, 30 x 22 in. © 1992 Sandra
Bowden. Used by permission.

Vault of the Four Seasons, Catacomb of Peter
and Marcellinus, Rome, Italy, early 4th century
Photo: Estelle Brettman, The International Catacomb
Society.

Derek Wadlington, *Baptismal Reflections*,
Campbell Hall Chapel of Columbia Theological Seminary,
Decatur, Georgia, 2005
Digital photograph (window reflection in font). Used by
permission of Derek Wadlington.

Alice Brinkman, *Burning Mystery*, 2003
Shibori dyed silk gauze and resist dyed cotton backdrop.
© 2003 Alice Brinkman. www.alicebrinkman.com

3:11

Elizabeth Steele Halstead, *The Tomb*, 2002

Oil on canvas, 30 x 30 in. © 2002 Elizabeth Steele Halstead. Used by permission.

Makoto Fujimura, *The White Tree*, 2000
48 x 60 in., Silver, Mineral Pigments, Oyster Shell White on Canvas. © Makoto Fujimura, 2000.

3:12-14 Unpacking the Mystery

Martin Bulinya, *On the March 2*
Acrylic and ink on paper, 6 x 17 3/4 in. From the collection of Elizabeth Steele Halstead.

M. J. Anderson, *Witness: Women of the Resurrection*, Church of the Resurrection, Solon, Ohio, 2005
Carrara marble bas relief diptych, 7' x 9' x 2'. © 2005 M. J. Anderson. Photo by Mary Ojnik. www.mjandersonsculpture.com

Michelangelo Merisi da Caravaggio, *Incredulity of Saint Thomas*, 1601-02
Caravaggio (Michelangelo Merisi da) (1573-1610). (Copy after). Incredulity of Saint Thomas. Uffizi, Florence, Italy. Photo Credit: SCALA / Art Resource, NY.

Communion of Saints, Cathedral of Our Lady of the Angels, Los Angeles, California, 2001-02
Cotton and viscose tapestries designed by John R. Nava. Woven by Flanders Tapestries. www.olacathedral.org/cathedral_art/tapestries.html

3:15-21 Eager Hope

Patricia Nix, *Tool*, 2001
Oil and Collage on Canvas, 60 x 35.5 in. Used by Permission. www.patricianix.com

Hieronymus Bosch, *The Prodigal Son*, 1500-1502
Bosch, Hieronymus (c.1450-1516). The Prodigal Son. Museum Boymans van Beuningen, Rotterdam, The Netherlands. Photo Credit: Kavaler / Art Resource, NY.

Edvard Munch, *The Scream*, 1893

Munch, Edvard (1863-1944). The Scream. 1893. (Tempera and pastels on cardboard, 91 x 73.5 cm). National Gallery, Oslo, Norway. © 2009 The Munch Museum / The Munch-Ellingsen Group / Artists Rights Society (ARS), New York. Photo Credit: Erich Lessing / Art Resource, NY.

Roger M. Varland, *Cain and Abel*, 1996
Silver print (black-and-white photograph), 19 x 13 in. © 1996 Roger M. Varland. Used by permission.

3:20-21

Anneke Kaai, *Psalm 84*, 1996
Anneke Kaai, Psalm 84 (1996), acrylic and mixed media on plexiglas. From Anneke Kaai & Eugene Peterson, *The Psalms* (1999), 31. Used with permission. www.piquanteditions.com

William Grosvenor Congdon, *Ego sum*, 1961
Oil and gold leaf on plywood. Galleria Arte Pro Civitate Christiana-Assisi-Italy.

John August Swanson, *Festival of Lights*, 2000
Festival of Lights © 2000 by John August Swanson. Serigraph 30 3/4 x 24 in. www.JohnAugustSwanson.com. Los Angeles artist John August Swanson is noted for his finely detailed, brilliantly colored paintings and original prints. His works are found in the Smithsonian Institution's National Museum of American History, London's Tate Gallery, the Vatican Museum's Collection of Modern Religious Art, and the Bibliothèque Nationale, Paris. Full-color posters and cards of Mr. Swanson's work are available from the National Association for Hispanic Elderly.

4:1-7 In the Lord

4:1

Rachel Durfee, *Stand Firm*, 2000
Rachel Durfee, "Stand Firm", © 2000, color etching, 24 x 24 in., All Rights Reserved, Used by Permission of the Artist.

Mala Sikka, *Touching Rocks*, 2004
Photograph by Mala Sikka, from 'The Ecodaya Island Sanctuary' situated alongside the Thungabhadra River near the ancient ruins of the World Heritage Site of

Hampi, located in Karnataka State/India.
www.ecodaya.net

4:2-3

Karyn Percival, *Searching for the Peacemaker*
Acrylic on canvas, 24 x 30 in. Used by permission of Ardill family.

Henri Matisse, *Dance (I)*, 1909
Matisse, Henri (1869-1954). Dance (I). Paris, Hôtel Biron, early 1909. Oil on canvas, 8' 6 1/2" x 12' 9 1/2" (259.7 x 390.1 cm). Gift of Nelson A. Rockefeller in honor of Alfred H. Barr, Jr. (210.1963). The Museum of Modern Art, New York, NY, U.S.A. © 2009 Succession H. Matisse / Artists Rights Society (ARS), New York. Digital Image © The Museum of Modern Art / Licensed by SCALA / Art Resource, NY.

4:4-5

Martin Bulinya, *Untitled*
Acrylic and ink on paper, 8 1/2 x 12 1/4 in. From the collection of Elizabeth Steele Halstead.

Henri Matisse, *Maquette for Nuit de Noël*, 1952
Matisse, Henri (1869-1954). Maquette for Nuit de Noël. Nice-Cimiez, Hôtel Régina, early 1952. Gouache on cut-and-pasted paper, homasote panel, 10' 7" x 53 1/2". Gift of Time Inc. (421.1953.1-5). The Museum of Modern Art, New York, NY, U.S.A. © 2009 Succession H. Matisse / Artists Rights Society (ARS), New York. Digital Image © The Museum of Modern Art / Licensed by SCALA / Art Resource, NY.

4:6

Laura James, *Love One Another*, 2000
Acrylics on canvas. © 2000 Laura James. Used by permission. *www.laurajamesart.com*

4:7

Vincent van Gogh, *The Good Samaritan (after Delacroix)*, 1890
Oil on canvas, 73 x 59.5 cm. Collection Kröller-Müller Museum, Otterlo, The Netherlands.

Ann Boyer LePere, *Sheltered*, 2004
© 2004 Ann Boyer LePere. Used by permission. *www.annboyerlepere.com*

4:8-9 Focused Praise

4:8-9

Timothy R. Botts, *Philippians 4:8*, 2000
Calligraphy. *The Holy Bible, Botts Illustrated Edition*, Tyndale, 2000. Calligraphy by Timothy R. Botts. Used by permission.

Cornelis Monsma, *Fruitful (Psalm 1:1-3)*, 2003
Oil on canvas, 80 x 100 cm (32 x 40 in.). © 2003 Cornelis Monsma. Used by permission. *www.monsmart.com*

Wassily Kandinsky, *Allerheiligen I (All Saints I)*, 1911
Allerheiligen I (All Saints I). Oil on glass, 34.5 x 40.5 cm. Städtische Galerie im Lenbachhaus, Munich. © 2009 Artists Rights Society (ARS), New York / ADAGP, Paris.

4:10-20 Contentment

4:10-13

Vincent van Gogh, *The potato-eaters*, 1885
Gogh, Vincent van (1853-1890). The potato-eaters. 1885. Rijksmuseum Kroeller-Mueller, Otterlo, The Netherlands. Photo Credit: Erich Lessing / Art Resource, NY.

Dejan Novcic, *Ballerina's Soles*
DIOMEDIA / Alamy

Watanabe Sadao, *The Last Supper*, 1981
Katazome print, 24 3/4 x 37 1/2 in. From the collection of Anne H.H. Pyle. By permission of Watanabe Harue. Image courtesy of the Museum of Biblical Art, New York City. Photo: Eduardo Calderón.

4:18

Vitali Komarov, *Peach Tree Orchard*, 2001
Oil on canvas. © 2001 Vitali Komarov. Used by permission. *www.komarovart.com*

Annie Vallotton, *The Woman Anointing Jesus' Feet*, 1976
Illustration by noted Swiss artist and storyteller, Annie Vallotton. Used by permission.

Cullen Washington, *Praising*, 2003

© Cullen Washington, 'Praising', Watercolor, 2003.
www..AllTribesArts.com

Joan Bohlig, *On the Table, Fruit*, 2005
Oil on canvas, 30 x 40 in. © 2005 Joan Bohlig. Used by permission. www.bohliggraphics.com

Banquet Scene, Catacomb of St. Callixtus, Rome, Italy, first half 3rd century
Photo: Estelle Brettman, The International Catacomb Society.

4:21-23 Grace and Peace

Icon of SS Peter and Paul
Tempera on panel. The London Art Archive / Alamy

Amanda Patrick, *Peace on Earth*, 2005
© Amanda Patrick, 'Peace on Earth', Ink & Watercolor, 2005. www..AllTribesArts.com

Anneke Kaai, *Grace*, 2003
Anneke Kaai, *Grace* (2003), acrylic on plexiglas. From Anneke Kaai & Eugene Peterson, *In a Word* (2003), 11. Used with permission. www.piquanteditions.com

Name Index

Title Index

Subject Index of Texts

282

Subject Index of Images

This topical index of images is based on the editor's interpretation of the artworks. We encourage you to make your own interpretative judgments, based on your context, and to expand on the list of pieces that reflect the message of Philippians.

Scripture Index